The Kindle Fire
PocketGuide

Scott **McNulty**

Ginormous knowledge, pocket-sized.

**Peachpit
Press**

The Kindle Fire Pocket Guide
Scott McNulty

Peachpit Press
1249 Eighth Street
Berkeley, CA 94710
510/524-2178
510/524-2221 (fax)

Find us on the Web at: www.peachpit.com
To report errors, please send a note to errata@peachpit.com.

Peachpit Press is a division of Pearson Education.

Editors: Cliff Colby, Kim Wimpsett
Production editor: Katerina Malone
Compositor: David Van Ness
Indexer: Valerie Haynes Perry
Cover design: Aren Straiger
Interior design: Peachpit Press

ISBN-13:   978-0-321-82016-7
ISBN-10:   0-321-82016-9

9 8 7 6 5 4 3 2 1

Printed and bound in the United States of America

*For all the people who dream impossible things
and share them with the rest of us.*

Acknowledgments

Thanks to all the engineers and magicians at Amazon for thinking up, and then actually making, the Kindle, without which this book would make little sense. I've spent many enjoyable hours using various Kindles, and it is always a pleasure.

The amazing folks at Peachpit have, once again, managed to shape my words into a pleasing, and useful, book. Thanks to Cliff Colby for steering the ship that is this book and to Kim Wimpsett for her editing prowess. My thanks to Katerina Malone for managing the production process, to David Van Ness for laying out this book, and to Valerie Haynes Perry for indexing.

As always, though many people helped to make this book a reality, any errors are mine alone.

About the Author

Scott McNulty owns more Kindles than is entirely sensible. Author of *The Kindle Pocket Guide,* devoted to the second-generation Kindle, he is known for his in-depth knowledge of, and enthusiasm for, the Kindle platform. Scott lives in Philadelphia with his wife, Marisa. By day he works at the Wharton School of the University of Pennsylvania, and by night he blogs about whatever strikes his fancy at *http://blog.blankbaby.com*. He has also been known to tweet once or twice under the handle *@blankbaby*.

Contents

1

Meet the Kindle Fire

I've bought myself every Kindle that Amazon has sold over the years, and the Kindle Fire is no exception (**Figure 1.1** on the next page). It is, however unlike any Kindle that has come before it. Right off the bat there is one clear difference: the screen. The Kindle Fire sports a vibrant, full-color, 7-inch display capable of multitouch gestures. With a fancy screen like that, it would be a crime to limit the Kindle Fire to being a simple e-reader. Good thing this isn't the case; unlike its predecessors, this Kindle isn't devoted to one task.

Figure 1.1
The Amazon Kindle Fire wants you to touch it.

The Fire is geared toward consuming media of all types. Of course, you can read any Kindle book on the Fire, but you can also do so much more: watch movies, read magazines, listen to your music, look at pictures, and install applications (called *apps*) that add even more functionality. Oddly enough, all of the content that the Kindle Fire enables you to consume can be purchased from Amazon. Furthermore, in true Amazon fashion, Amazon makes it very easy to spend your money on all those books, movies, and apps right from the Fire, which is great for both you and Amazon.

note You aren't restricted to Amazon-purchased content on your Kindle Fire; you can fill it up easily with e-books and movies that you already have.

Nowhere on Amazon.com will you see the Kindle Fire referred to as a *tablet*, and yet that's exactly what it is. Chances are you'll be comparing the Fire to other tablets on the market, so you'll need to know what it does and doesn't offer. It is the only tablet completely integrated with

Amazon services (more on that in a second). It will connect to Wi-Fi networks; however, it doesn't include a 3G or 4G wireless radio, which means if you're not within range of Wi-Fi, your Fire isn't going to connect to the Web (though it also means you don't need to pay for another wireless data plan). The Fire also lacks a camera of any kind (front-facing or rear-facing), so you won't be using it to video conference or snap pictures. However, the price of the Fire is amazingly low when you consider how well the device is made. (There are cheaper tablets out there, but they look and feel very, very cheap. The Fire feels great in your hand and has a very solid build.) Also, there is a huge array of content available for it.

Why would you get a Fire? If you're a big user of Amazon services (I buy almost everything I can from Amazon; I even use Amazon's Subscribe and Save to automatically send me a huge box of toilet paper every six months), then the Kindle Fire is the tablet for you, doubly so if you are a member of Amazon Prime (**Figure 1.2**).

Figure 1.2
*The Amazon
Prime logo*

Amazon Prime is a membership program that costs $79 for a yearly enrollment. That $79 gets you, and up to four family members, free two-day shipping on any Amazon Prime item (denoted by an Amazon Prime logo) on Amazon.com (**Figure 1.3**). Amazon Prime members can also upgrade to overnight shipping on eligible items for $3.99 per item. That's not a bad deal if you're a frequent Amazon buyer. However, what does this have to do with the Kindle Fire, other than impact the shipping on the device?

Figure 1.3
*This logo means
the item is Prime
eligible.*

In addition to the shipping benefits, Amazon has been adding other goodies for Amazon Prime members. The two newest features of Amazon Prime seem designed for the Kindle Fire: Prime Instant Videos and the Kindle Owners' Lending Library.

Amazon Instant Video is a section of Amazon.com that features a number of movies and TV shows that you can stream and purchase. Amazon Prime members can stream a subset of these videos for free as often as they like. This is the service called Prime Instant Videos (**Figure 1.4**).

Figure 1.4
Thousands of streaming videos are available to Prime members.

Much like Netflix, you can watch as many of the streaming videos as you like a month on a variety of devices. Prime Instant Videos can be watched through a web browser, on certain Blu-ray players, on an HDTV with a Roku (*www.roku.com*), or on your Kindle Fire. No additional charge is required for these videos, and since they're streaming, they don't take up any space on your devices. All you need is an Internet connection, an Amazon Prime membership, and a desire to watch some movies or TV shows (including all the *Star Trek* series) (**Figure 1.5**).

tip Check out this list of Amazon Instant Video–compatible devices to see whether you own any additional devices that support Amazon videos: *www.amazon.com/gp/video/ontv/devices*.

Figure 1.5
TV shows usually include multiple seasons.

The Kindle Owners' Lending Library was added to Amazon Prime in early November 2011 just a couple of weeks before the Fire shipped (**Figure 1.6**). If you are a Kindle device owner (either a Kindle Fire or an e-ink Kindle) with a Prime membership, you can "borrow" one book a month from the Kindle Owners' Lending Library directly on your Kindle (you can't borrow books using Amazon's website or one of the free Kindle apps for smartphones and tablets other than the Fire). These books offer the same features any other Kindle book does including syncing your notes and highlights across your devices. The only difference is at the end of the month you can no longer access the book on your Kindle (though your notes and highlights are still available if you buy the book for yourself).

Figure 1.6
The Kindle Owners' Lending Library allows you to borrow a Kindle book from a selected list for a month.

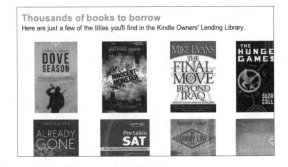

At the moment, there are thousands of books to choose from, including some *New York Times* best sellers; however, none of the major publishers has signed on for the service at the time I'm writing this. Still, this is a perk that will become more valuable over time as the lendable book selection grows.

Amazon thinks that Amazon Prime is such a critical component of using a Fire that a free month of Prime is included with each Fire purchase. The month starts the moment you turn on your registered Fire. At the end of the month, you'll be asked whether you would like to sign up for Prime for a year. (If it isn't clear by now, I recommend you take advantage of Prime. You'll earn back the $79 in shipping savings alone.)

A Tablet by Any Other Name

As I mentioned, Amazon never calls the Kindle Fire a tablet, but that's exactly what it is. It is running Google's mobile operating system called Android, but you wouldn't know that unless someone (like me) told you. Amazon has taken the time to completely customize the user interface of the Fire, making it unlike any Android tablet on the market. But does the world need another tablet? The world may not need one, but I am grateful that Amazon created the Fire because of its killer feature: deep Amazon integration. Using all the Amazon services you know and love is effortless with the Fire.

Fire vs. iPad

It would be remiss of me if I didn't mention the Kindle Fire's biggest competitor: Apple's iPad. Many people seem to think that it is an either-or situation: Buy a Fire or buy an iPad. Both tablets have very different takes on the mobile computing experience. The iPad tries to be all things to everyone, with thousands of apps. The Fire has many apps available to it, that's true, but consuming media is the star here. I like to think of the Fire as a straw through which I can drink the seemingly unending amount of content that Amazon has to offer.

Fire or iPad? I say, why not both?

Touching Fire

The Kindle Fire is an all-touch, all-the-time device. You won't be using a mouse or keyboard to interact with your Fire. All you need are a couple of fingers, and you can operate the Kindle Fire like a pro.

I said a couple of fingers because the Fire sports a multitouch display. It knows when you have more than one finger touching the display, which allows for a number of gestures that just weren't possible before multi-touch technology became so prevalent.

The first thing you need to know is the *swipe*. When you turn on your Kindle Fire, you're be greeted with a lock screen and instructions to swipe along the unlock bar to access the device (**Figure 1.7** on the next page). To swipe, just press your finger against the screen and rapidly drag it left or right: Those are left and right swipes, respectively (to unlock the screen, you have to use a left swipe).

Figure 1.7
Swipe along the orange line to unlock your Fire for the first time.

Whenever you need to touch something on the screen quickly with a finger, I will call that a *tap*. For example, when you want to use the Fire's keyboard, you tap each key one at a time.

Holding your finger against an on-screen element for a couple of seconds is called a *long tap*. Think of the long tap as the touch interface's equivalent of the right-click. This is how you access secondary functions, such as getting more information about a song in the music player.

You can move things around on the Kindle Fire's screen by long tapping and dragging your finger against the screen. In some screens, like the home screen, the item you long tapped will move along with your finger so you can place it elsewhere.

Throughout the book I'll describe sequences of taps that you'll need to do in order to accomplish something. I will write them in a sequence like so: Books > Store > Bestsellers. This means:

- Tap Books in the Navigation bar.
- In the Books section, tap Store.
- Once in the Store, tap Bestsellers.

When you're looking at pictures or reading a website, you might want to zoom in to get a better look. The Fire offers two gestures that allow you to zoom: the *double tap* and *pinch*. Double tapping is pretty straightforward: Tap twice in rapid succession on something you want to zoom in on (this works best in the Fire's web browser on a column of text or an image), and the Fire will zoom in automatically.

Pinching allows you greater control over the zoom level, since you decide when to stop. Put your index finger and thumb together on the screen and separate them to zoom in; to zoom out, move them back together.

The Kindle Fire is light enough to be held with one hand, but don't be afraid to grip it with both. Two hands become very helpful when you're typing on the keyboard or tapping icons across the screen. An errant tap won't do any damage to your Fire, so feel free to get up-close and personal with it.

Your First Kindle Fire Moments

As soon as you take your Kindle Fire out of its box, you'll notice a couple things right off the bat. The only things in the box are the Kindle Fire, a charger, and a very brief Quick Start Guide (**Figure 1.8**).

Figure 1.8

The Fire doesn't come with much: the device, a power adapter, and a Quick Start Guide.

The Kindle Fire is a rectangle almost entirely devoted to the 7-inch screen. Holding the Kindle Fire in one hand is easy because it weighs only a little more than a full can of your favorite soda (for those of you into exact measurements, the Fire weighs 14.6 ounces). At 7.5 by 4.7 inches, the Kindle Fire will easily fit into a backpack, purse, or large jacket pocket. Don't worry about accidentally scratching the display, though, because it is made of Gorilla Glass, a very resilient type of glass that is tough to scratch. If you don't want to risk any damage to your Fire, Amazon does sell a number of cases to protect your investment a little, and some even include stands so you can set up your Fire on a table and have a nice viewing angle for watching videos.

As you look at the front of the Fire, you'll see that it has a "chin" of sorts (**Figure 1.9**). This really stands out when the Fire is held in portrait mode (the screen is taller than it is wide). The chin is the bottom of the device, while the skinnier part will be referred to as the top of the Kindle.

Figure 1.9
The bottom edge of the Fire is wider than the top.

note You can use your Fire in either landscape (the screen is held so it is wider than it is tall) or portrait during most activities. The Fire automatically rotates the screen for you when you turn the device, but it is clear after using it for a while that Amazon really thinks you should use it in portrait mode for most uses. It is your choice, though; most functions will work fine in either orientation (video will be played only in landscape, though).

Figure 1.10
The power button, head-phone jack, and micro-USB port are all located on the bottom of the device.

Along the bottom edge of your Fire you'll find a power button, the headphone jack, and a micro-USB 2 port (this is the same port found on every Kindle that Amazon has produced thus far) (**Figure 1.10**). The head-phone jack accepts any standard 3.5mm headphones, so you can rock out to your music or listen to a movie with a little privacy. If you want to share your audio with the world, the Kindle Fire has two speakers located at the top of the device.

The micro-USB port serves double duty as a way to recharge the device and to add your own content. Plug the included power adapter into a standard outlet and then slide the end connector into the micro-USB port to charge your Kindle. Charging your Kindle fully should take about 4 hours, and the battery will give you about 8 hours of reading time and 7.5 hours of continuous video playback with wireless off. If you're browsing the Web or doing anything else that requires an active Internet connection, the battery time will vary.

You can also charge your Fire by connecting it to a computer, but the cable required for that is not included in the box. To charge your Fire via your computer, you need to buy a micro-USB cable, and your computer must have a powered USB port. (Most USB ports that are physically located on a computer tend to be powered; if you want to charge your Fire using a USB hub, make sure it says it is a powered USB hub.)

Figure 1.11

When connected to a computer, your Fire's screen declares it is in USB Drive Mode.

When you plug your Fire into a port on a computer, it goes into USB mode (**Figure 1.11**). This allows you to simply drag and drop your own files onto the Fire. Those files then show up when you're using the device. Keep in mind only a limited number of file types are supported, and those files need to be placed in the correct directory in order to be readable.

The power button is the only physical button on the entire device. Press the power button to turn on your Fire. The button glows with a green light when the Fire is starting. When you want to turn off your Fire's screen, just press the power button, and your Fire goes to sleep. Waking it up requires another press of the power button. If you need to turn it off completely (perhaps on a plane), just hold the power button down for a few seconds until the Fire shuts down (**Figure 1.12**).

Figure 1.12
Holding down the power button brings up your shutdown options.

There is a chance that your Kindle Fire might freeze while doing something. No piece of technology is perfect, which is why there is a way to force your Fire to reboot. Press and hold the power button for 20 seconds; the screen will flicker, and the device will reboot (ideally solving whatever problem you might have encountered).

Firing Up Your Fire for the First Time

There's no need for a computer to set up your new Kindle. All you need is the Fire, an Internet connection, and an Amazon account to register it (and if your Kindle is preregistered, you might not even need that). Even updates to the Kindle Fire's software are performed on the device itself.

When purchased directly from Amazon.com, the Kindle Fire is registered to whatever Amazon account was used to purchase it. All your Amazon content appears on the Fire automatically when you turn it on for the first time (which is very neat). If you're purchasing this Fire as a gift or at a retail location like Radio Shack, it won't be associated with any Amazon account (see the sidebar "Giving the Gift of Fire" for details on how to buy the Fire as a gift), and you'll have to manually associate your new Fire with your account.

Giving the Gift of Fire

What happens if you want to buy someone a Kindle Fire as a present? First, you give great gifts! Second, when you're ordering the Kindle Fire from Amazon.com, make sure to check "This will be a gift" on the Fire's product page (**Figure 1.13**). (Fires purchased from a retail location are sold unregistered, so there's no need to tell the store you've giving this Fire as a gift unless you like sharing.) This will tell the elves at Amazon not to register this Fire to your Amazon account.

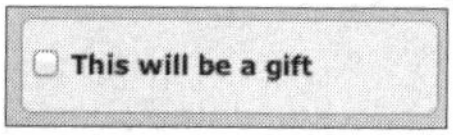

☐ **This will be a gift**

Figure 1.13

Selecting this box when ordering a Kindle Fire from Amazon will ensure it isn't registered to your Amazon account.

Take the Fire out of the box and press the power button for a couple of seconds. The Welcome to Kindle Fire screen appears. Right off the bat you're able to join your Kindle Fire to any available Wi-Fi networks in range (**Figure 1.14**). You can skip this step by tapping "Complete later," but a Fire without a network connection isn't much fun, so let's just set it up now.

You're presented with a list of Wi-Fi networks that the Fire can see. If your Wi-Fi network's name is in the list, select it by tapping it. Enter a username and password, if required by the Wi-Fi network, and the Fire is connected.

Your wireless network might not be listed in the Available Networks section. Fear not, that probably means your network isn't set up to broadcast its name to all devices. (This is a little more secure because not only do people need to have a username and password to connect to the network, but they need to know the name of the network as well.) You can manually enter your network's name by tapping Other Network.

Figure 1.14

Choose the correct Wi-Fi network from the list.

tip Tap a field where you would like to input text, and the Kindle Keyboard appears at the bottom of the screen. If you need to enter numbers and letters (as might be the case for your Wi-Fi password), notice that the top row of letters has numbers in the upper-right corner of each key. If you long tap one of those keys, the number appears so you can enter it instead of the letter (**Figure 1.15**).

Figure 1.15

Long tapping the top row of letter keys gives you access to the number keys.

Figure 1.16

The "Enter other Wi-Fi network" screen allows you to manually join a Wi-Fi network that doesn't broadcast its name.

The "Enter other Wi-Fi network" setup screen asks for the SSID, or name, of the wireless network you want to join (**Figure 1.16**). Tap the field and type in the name using the on-screen keyboard. Tap OK, and then tap the Security drop-down menu to select whatever security scheme your wireless network uses (if you aren't sure, ask whoever set up the wireless network). If you select a security level that requires a username and password, those fields now appear, so fill them in.

Tap OK to proceed to the next step, or tap Cancel to go back to the Available Networks screen.

Once you've joined a wireless network, you get to set your time zone. Tap the correct entry in the list (**Figure 1.17**). At the moment, the Kindle Fire is being sold in the United States only, so international time zones aren't listed on the main screen, but you can access a full list of available time zones by tapping Select Another.

Tap Continue.

Figure 1.17
Pick a time zone, any time zone.

At this point, one of two things will happen:

- The Welcome to Fire screen congratulates you and displays a Get Started Now button (**Figure 1.18**). This happens if your Kindle Fire is already registered to your Amazon account (i.e., you purchased it from Amazon with the account you intend to use with it).

Figure 1.18
The final setup screen. Tap Get Started Now to use your Kindle Fire.

- If the Kindle isn't preregistered to an account because it was a gift (see the sidebar "Giving the Gift of Fire"), because you purchased it at a retail location, or because you've reset the Fire to its default settings, you'll need to register it to an account before you can do anything.

Enter your Amazon username (the e-mail address you use to log into Amazon's website) and password on the Register Your Kindle screen (**Figure 1.19**). You can tap "Show password" in case you have a complicated password and you want to double-check your typing. Once you're sure you have the correct information entered, tap Register, and the Fire will register itself with your Amazon account.

Figure 1.19
If your Kindle isn't registered, enter your Amazon account information.

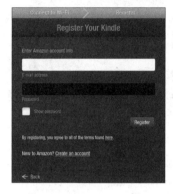

note The registering process requires the Fire to be connected to the Internet, so if you skipped the Wi-Fi setup earlier, you'll need to complete that before you can register your Kindle Fire.

If someone you know gave you a Kindle Fire and you've never used Amazon.com, welcome back from whatever place you've been for the last decade (I kid, I kid). You can create an Amazon account right from the Fire (this requires an Internet connection as well).

Figure 1.20

Don't have an Amazon account? You can create one right on the Fire.

On the Register screen (shown in Figure 1.19), tap New to Amazon? to go to the Create an Amazon Account screen (**Figure 1.20**). Type your name, your e-mail address, and a password twice (make sure it's a good one). Tap Continue, and your Amazon account is created.

After you register your Kindle Fire to your existing, or newly created, Amazon account, the final Welcome screen is displayed (shown in Figure 1.18). I didn't mention it, but if this Kindle Fire is registered to the wrong account somehow, you can take care of that here too. Tap the Not Scott? link (though it'll display whatever name is associated with the Amazon account the Fire is registered to), and that will start the deregistration process so you register it to the proper account.

Once you're ready to get started, tap "Get started now."

The Kindle Fire Home Screen

The first time you see your Fire's home screen, an overlaid tutorial appears pointing out various parts of the interface (**Figure 1.21**). Tap Next to go through the three screens of the tutorial. Tap Close on the final screen to start using your Fire.

Figure 1.21

The startup tutorial quickly points out sections of your Fire.

You're going to spend a fair amount of time here on the Fire home screen. Nearly every time you want to switch to another book, launch an app, or start watching a movie, you'll end up interacting with a particular section of the home screen. It is broken up into a number of different sections: the status bar, the Search box, the Navigation bar, the Carousel, and Favorites (**Figure 1.22**).

Figure 1.22
The Kindle Fire home screen

Status bar

Search box

Navigation bar

Carousel

Favorites

Status Bar

The status bar runs along the top of edge of the Fire's screen and remains visible while you're doing most things on your Fire (**Figure 1.23**). It is hidden when you're watching a movie, reading a book, or using certain apps, but you can make it visible at any point by tapping the screen.

Figure 1.23 *The status bar displays nuggets of useful information.*

At the left of the status bar is the name of your Kindle Fire, which is usually [your first name]'s Kindle. If you've owned more than one Kindle in your life (I'm on my ninth or tenth), then the naming scheme changes to [your first names]'s *x*th Kindle where *x* denotes the number of Kindle this one is.

This area is also used to display notifications (**Figure 1.24**). Notifications alert you when something has happened on your Kindle Fire. For instance, if you have an e-mail client installed, it'll use notifications to tell you when a new message has arrived. Games use notifications to let you know when someone has challenged you to a new game, and so on.

Figure 1.24
The number of pending notifications are displayed next to your Kindle's name.

The number of pending notifications is displayed next to your Fire's name (shown in Figure 1.24). Tap the number to expand the notification tray (**Figure 1.25**). The tray gathers notifications into two groups: ongoing notifications (at the bottom) and plain old notifications. No matter which group the notification falls into, an icon of the app/process that sent the notification is displayed along with the text of the notification.

Figure 1.25
Tap the notification number to expand the notification tray.

Ongoing notifications let you know about processes that are currently underway, such as the checking of an e-mail account or the progress of an app install, for instance. The top group displays things that have already happened and need you either to interact with or to just be aware of.

Tapping an alert takes you to whatever app created the alert and removes the notification from the tray. If you want to clear all the notifications at once, just tap the "Clear all" button, and both groups of notifications will be cleared.

 If your Fire's volume isn't muted, you'll also hear a sound every time a new notification appears.

Smack dab in the middle of the status bar is the current time. On the right side of the status bar you'll see three icons: Quick Settings, the Wi-Fi signal strength, and the battery indicator.

The Wi-Fi signal strength and battery indicators work just like they do on any other device. The Wi-Fi indicator shows you how strong the wireless signal is: The more bars, the better. If you've connected to a wireless connection that requires web-based authentication, like in a Starbucks or hotel, the indicator will show the strength but also display an *X*. Launch the web browser (more on that later) to load the authentication page and join the wireless network.

The battery indicator (which looks like a battery) lets you know how much juice your Fire has left (**Figure 1.26**). The more the battery is filled in with white, the more power you have left. When you have the Fire's power adapter plugged into the USB port on the bottom of the device, the icon animates and fills with green to indicate it is charging.

Figure 1.26
The battery icon changes when the Fire is charging, when the battery isn't full, and when your charge is very low.

When your battery is getting a little too low, the indicator turns red. When you're really running down the battery, a warning pops up telling you that you need to charge your Fire before it shuts itself down. If you ignore that warning, your Kindle Fire will shut itself off (**Figure 1.27**). Connect it to the charger for a few minutes, and you should be able to turn it back on.

Figure 1.27
Before your Kindle shuts itself down because of low power, it warns you.

As the device is charging, the light on the power button will glow red. It turns green when the Kindle Fire has been fully charged.

Tapping the Quick Settings icon (that's the gear icon) brings up a few commonly used settings in one convenient place (**Figure 1.28**). Let's take a look at what each of those settings do from left to right:

Figure 1.28
Quick Settings gives you access to commonly used functions at a tap.

- *Lock/Unlock*: In most areas of the Fire, when you rotate the device from portrait to landscape, the screen automatically rotates to reflect the way you're holding it. This way, you don't end up trying to read a book sideways. Sometimes the autorotating screen can be annoying. Tap the Lock icon to lock the screen's orientation to the current orientation. The icon changes from an open lock to a closed lock, and now no matter how you move your Fire, the screen won't budge (**Figure 1.29**). When you're ready to turn it back on, tap the Unlock icon and autorotation returns.

Figure 1.29
The screen orientation is locked. It won't change no matter how the device is held.

- *Volume*: Many types of content on the Kindle Fire have the ability to make noise: music, movies, apps, and even some books and magazines that incorporate video or sounds. Since the Fire lacks physical volume buttons, the engineers at Amazon made sure that your volume controls are always a single tap away. Whenever you tap the Quick Settings icon, the volume controls are displayed by default (**Figure 1.30**). Press your finger on the slider, and slide up to increase the volume and down to lower it. You can also tap the area on the slider you want to set the volume, and it will jump to that point.

Figure 1.30
The Kindle Fire volume slider

When you're listening to music on your Fire, the Volume control becomes even more useful. In addition to controlling the volume of the music, play controls and some information about the currently playing track are displayed (**Figure 1.31**). You can pause the song and skip ahead or back right from here, no matter what else you're doing on your Fire.

Figure 1.31
When music is playing, playback controls are displayed in addition to the slider.

- *Brightness*: The Fire's screen is pretty bright, which makes it great for watching movies. Tapping the Brightness icon allows you to increase or decrease the screen's brightness by sliding your finger up or down (**Figure 1.32**).

Figure 1.32
Screen brightness is controlled by the Kindle itself by default. Turn this off to manually set your screen's brightness.

- *Wi-Fi*: As you might expect, the Wi-Fi settings allow you to determine which network your Kindle Fire is connected to, much as you did during the initial setup process (**Figure 1.33**). At the top of the Wi-Fi settings is a toggle button that allows you to completely turn off wireless and turn it back on (and vice versa). You might consider doing this if you are in a place where Wi-Fi isn't available; it will conserve battery life.

Figure 1.33

These Wi-Fi options should look familiar if you've recently set up your Kindle Fire.

Under the on/off toggle you'll find the list of Wi-Fi networks your Fire can currently see. Swipe down with your finger to scroll through the list if there are many available networks. Tap the name of a network to see more details about it (**Figure 1.34**). From here you can connect to this network, have your Fire "forget" this network so it will never use it, and see the selected network's signal strength (stronger is better) and Link Speed (faster is better). If you want to connect to this network, tap Connect.

Figure 1.34

Details about an available Wi-Fi network. You can even join this network from here with a tap.

Back in the list of available networks, if you scroll to the bottom, you'll see two options: Advanced Settings and Add a Network (**Figure 1.35**). Tap Add a Network to add a wireless network to your Kindle that isn't listed. You'll need to enter the network's name (SSID), the security type, and a username/password if required.

Figure 1.35
Advanced Settings and Add a Net-work are always at the bottom of the available wireless networks list.

The Advanced Settings option allows you to do two things: enable international channels and assign a static IP address to your Fire (**Figure 1.36**). What the heck does all that mean? I've mentioned before that the Kindle Fire is available only in the United States at the moment, but that doesn't mean you can't take it with you to another country (or have one of your clever U.S. friends buy one for you and ship it to your home country). While in countries outside of America, you might need to connect to a Wi-Fi network that operates on a chan-nel not supported in the United States. (The spectrum that Wi-Fi uses is divided up into a number of channels, and the channels are all stan-dard, but some countries have regulations that require channels that other countries don't.) "Enable International channels" will allow your Kindle Fire to recognize, search for, and join Wi-Fi networks using those channels not used in America.

Figure 1.36

Assigning your Fire a static IP address is an option many people won't need to take advantage of, but it is nice to have.

Tapping Static IP address takes you to a screen that asks for a bunch of networking information, including the IP address you want to assign to your Kindle Fire (**Figure 1.37**). If you have no idea what any of this means, chances are you won't need to bother with this feature. The vast majority of wireless networks are set up to assign any device that connects to them an IP address (a unique address that the network uses to communicate with the device) automatically.

Figure 1.37

If none of these settings makes any sense to you, chances are you don't need to set an IP address for your Fire.

- *Sync*: Part of the secret sauce to Amazon's Kindle success has been WhisperSync, which keeps track of where you are in a book from Kindle to Kindle. You can start a book on an e-ink Kindle, open it in the Kindle app on your smartphone, and start right where you left off. WhisperSync is also incorporated into the Kindle Fire. Tapping Sync will force your Kindle Fire to sync with Amazon's servers and update your current location in your books, update your place in any Amazon instant streaming videos you might be watching, download any apps/Kindle books that you may have purchased on Amazon.com, and sync with any new music you either added to your Amazon Cloud player or bought from the Amazon MP3 store.

note WhisperSync also syncs any notes, highlights, and bookmarks you add to Kindle books and personal documents across your devices.

- *More*: The five settings listed in the Quick Settings don't cover nearly every setting on your Kindle Fire. Tap the More icon to see a list of all the settings that you probably won't need daily access to (**Figure 1.38**). Here you can turn off the keypress sound on your Kindle keyboard (More > Kindle Keyboard > Sound on keypress). You can also read the legal notices (More > Legal Notices) or determine your device's MAC address (More > Device > Wi-Fi MAC address).

Figure 1.38
This humble icon is the gateway to the rest of your Fire's settings.

If you're really stuck on something and don't want to turn to this book for help, you can also access help from the Settings section (More > Help & Feedback) (**Figure 1.39**). You can read the FAQ (frequently asked questions) and even request that an Amazon customer support rep call you so you can ask them about whatever issue you're having (related to the Kindle Fire, of course; Amazon customer support can't help you with your love life) (**Figure 1.40**).

Figure 1.39
The Help section is available to answer questions about your Kindle.

Figure 1.40
You can request to have an Amazon customer service person call you, right from the Fire.

This is just a small sampling of all the settings you'll find in the More section.

Search

Right below the status bar is the prominently featured Search box. Tap to activate it, and type in a query for your search. Once you enter a search term, the results from across all the content on your Fire and the Internet are returned in two lists (**Figure 1.41**).

Figure 1.41
Search results include items from across your Kindle and the cloud.

The search term is displayed at the top with two tabs: Library and Web. The Library tab, selected by default, displays all the things that were found on your Kindle. The Web lists results from the Internet.

As you can see, the results are grouped by content type: books with books, apps with apps, and so on, in the Library results. The most relevant matches are displayed at the top of their respective groups.

Each result is formatted in pretty much the same way. To the left is an image representing the item: the book/magazine cover, the album cover, or the app's icon. This really helps to scan the results for the thing you're looking for quickly. More information about the item is displayed next to the thumbnail image.

The item's name is displayed at the top with the author's name, artist's name, or date of publication underneath (depending on the content type). Both books and Docs (Docs are Kindle Fire talk for documents you add to your Fire from places other than Amazon) display your progress as a percentage so you know how far you've read. If the item is a new addition to your Kindle Fire, the New icon appears in the search results (**Figure 1.42**).

Figure 1.42
The New icon denotes newly added content.

Tap a result to open that item, whether it is a book, album, document, or app.

note Search searches across both the items you have on your device and those that are in Amazon's "cloud." In the case of books, this means any of your Kindle books in the "archive" that match your search will show up in the results. You'll know these books aren't on your device because their results include a download icon (**Figure 1.43**). Tapping that icon, or the search result itself, will download that book to your device and open it.

Figure 1.43
Tap the download icon to move this piece of content from the cloud to your device.

To view the search results from the Web, tap the Web tab (**Figure 1.44**). Much like the Library results, the web results are displayed in a list. Unlike the Library results, though, this list doesn't contain results of the search but rather suggested Google searches that might be related to your search string.

Figure 1.44
The Web tab lists possible Google searches based on your query.

Tapping any of the suggested search terms launches the Fire's web browser, called Silk, and presents you with a web page that is very familiar to anyone who has used the Internet in the past ten years: Google search results.

Navigation Bar

The Navigation bar allows you to view the various content libraries on your Fire and the Web (**Figure 1.45**). Tapping each entry on the Navigation bar will take you to the corresponding library on your Kindle Fire with a couple of exceptions (as noted):

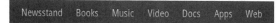

Figure 1.45 *The Navigation bar is how you get to the various libraries on your Fire.*

- *Newsstand*: All of your digital magazine and newspaper subscriptions will appear in your Newsstand library. This section also allows you to purchase additional subscriptions via the Newsstand store.

- *Books*: The Kindle has built its name by allowing you to read e-books, and the Fire is no different. Tap Books to see the full list of your books, as well as access the Kindle Store to buy more books. (Feel free to search for *Scott McNulty* and buy every book you find. Trust me, they're all excellent.)

- *Music*: Any music and playlists that are available on your Amazon Cloud Player can be accessed in your Fire's Music library. You can purchase MP3s here as well.

- *Video*: Unlike the other sections, the Video section defaults to display Amazon's instant streaming library. With a Prime membership, you have access to a large number of TV shows and movies, though you must be connected to a Wi-Fi network to stream video. As you're searching Amazon's video, you'll notice you can also purchase videos, which will be downloaded directly to your device. These videos are stored in the video library and can be watched at any point, whether you have a network connection or not.

- *Docs*: You can transfer personal documents—Word files, PDFs, text files, and more—to your Fire for reading. These documents are stored in the Docs library.

- *Apps*: The Apps library lists all the apps you have installed on your Kindle Fire arranged either in order of which they were lasted used or by title.

- *Web*: If you want to browse the Web, tap Web to be taken to the Fire's browser, Silk. On the surface, Silk functions very much like a standard web browser: Type in a URL or a search term to start browsing, and Silk will display the pages. Silk also supports bookmarks, so you can easily access pages you frequently visit. A lot more is actually going on behind the scenes with Silk; more information on what makes Silk so unique is in the "Browsing with Silk and the Cloud" section.

Figure 1.46

The Carousel displays all the content on your Kindle Fire.

Carousel

The most noticeable part of the Kindle Fire home screen is the Carousel (**Figure 1.46**). The Carousel is so named because it works very much like a merry-go-round you would find on any number of playgrounds. Instead of happily screaming children, this Carousel displays the items on your Kindle Fire in chronological order. The most recently interacted with items appear at the top of the Carousel, with older stuff stacked behind. When you first turn on your Kindle Fire, all of your Kindle books will be arrayed in the Carousel with the books you've most recently opened on top, and then the rest are shown in reverse purchase order (i.e., the books you bought most recently are displayed before older purchases).

Swipe your finger from the right to the left to advance through the Carousel. Swipe in the opposite direction to go the other way.

As you start to use your Fire to watch videos, read books, and install apps, the Carousel will become more interesting and useful. Whenever you access a book, video, or other type of content, an icon for it (i.e., the album cover or app icon) appears at the top of the Carousel. Recently visited websites are also displayed on the Carousel, so you can quickly go back to them.

Tapping any of the icons in the Carousel takes you to that piece of content whether it be a book or website.

If you stop the Carousel and display a book, you might notice a couple of icons appear on the cover. Here's what they mean:

- : When this appears on a book cover, that book isn't actually on your Kindle Fire but rather on Amazon's servers (also known as the *cloud*). Tapping the arrow icon initiates a download so you can read the book.

- : As a book downloads, a progress bar appears on the icon in the Carousel. This tracks how much of the book has been downloaded. Tap it to pause the download.

- : As soon as the book is downloaded, it is added to your device's book library. A New banner is also displayed on the upper-right corner of the book's Carousel icon. This goes away after you open the book for the first time.

- : After you've opened a book, a new icon appears: a bookmark. The bookmark lets you know that you've actually opened this book, and it displays how much of the book you've read as a percentage.

- : You can sample books before you buy them on the Kindle store. Each sample will sport this icon.

All of these icons take a second or two to appear in the Carousel, so you won't see them as you're swiping along; they appear only when you pause on a book.

At the moment, there is no way to "clear" your Carousel of any content, other than to delete it from your Kindle Fire. If you, for instance, visit a particular website in error, it will show up on your Carousel if that's the last thing you've visited in the web browser. You can always open a number of different things to "bury" Carousel items you don't want showing up as the topmost item.

Favorites

The final section of the Fire's home screen lists your Favorites **(Figure 1.47)**. You can add almost any type of content to your virtual Favorite's shelves right from the Carousel. Favorites act as shortcuts so you can jump directly to that app, magazine, album, or book without having to swipe through the Carousel or search the appropriate library.

Figure 1.47
Your Favorites are shortcuts to frequently used content, apps, and websites.

note Things in your Amazon cloud can be added to Favorites without needing to download them to your device. When you tap the Favorite, the Fire automatically downloads the content.

You can have as many Favorites as you like, and you can even organize them to your heart's content. As you start to add things to your Favorites, the shelves will extend below the edge of your screen. Swipe up with your finger to see the rest of your Favorites shelves, and swipe down to return to the Carousel.

You'll notice that Amazon thoughtfully added three apps to your Favorites:

- *Amazon app*: This app allows you to shop on Amazon.com for any number of things.

- *Pulse app*: You want to keep up on the news, and Pulse is a free app that presents news from *packs*, or groups of websites, in a fun and entertaining way.

Managing Favorites

Favorites can be added directly from the Carousel. Long tap the item you want to add, and a context menu will appear (**Figure 1.48**). Tap Add to Favorites, and that's it. The icon now appears both on the Favorites shelf and on the Carousel.

Figure 1.48
Long tapping items brings up the context menu, which offers options based on context. In this case, you can add this item to your Favorites.

If you decide you no longer want that item in your Favorites, it is easy to remove. Long tap one of your Favorites to bring up the context menu with one option: Remove from Favorites (**Figure 1.49**). Tap Remove from Favorites to delete this shortcut from your Favorites. The item isn't deleted from your Fire, just removed from Favorites. The item will still appear in the Carousel and the corresponding library.

Figure 1.49
Remove an item from Favorites by using the context menu.

(continues on next page)

Managing Favorites (continued)

Since Favorites appear in the Carousel in addition to the Favorites shelf, you can also remove them using the Carousel context menu. Long tap the item in the Carousel and tap Remove from Favorites. Look at the Favorites' shelf, and the icon is gone.

Once you have more than a handful of Favorites, you're going to want to arrange them in some order (I have my most used Favorites on the first shelf for easy access). Press your finger on the Favorite you want to move, and while keeping your finger pressed against the screen, move it to the place where you would like it to be (**Figure 1.50**). The other Favorites move out of the way to allow the icon to be placed where you want it.

Figure 1.50

Moving a Favorite to a new location

Once the Favorite is in the location you're after, just lift your finger, and the icon will stay there.

- *IMDB app*: IMDB, the Internet Movie Database, is your one-stop shop for all information Hollywood. Want to know who that guy was in that movie you watched was? The IMDB app is here to help.

- *Facebook app*: I bet you've heard of Facebook. This app is a link to Facebook's mobile website.

None of these apps is actually installed on your Fire; when you tap one to launch it, it is downloaded to your Fire and then launched.

Options Bar

You can find the options bar at the bottom of every screen, other than the home screen, on your Fire (**Figure 1.51**). As you might recall, the Fire has very few physical buttons, which means there needs to be software buttons in order to perform certain functions such as returning to the home screen and going back to a previous screen in an app.

Figure 1.51 *The options bar appears on every screen other than the home screen.*

The icons from left to right are as follows:

- ⌂ : Tap this button no matter where you are in the Fire to return to the home screen.

- ← : What this button does depends on what you're doing. If you've just entered into one of the content libraries, like Books for example, tapping Back will bring you back to the home screen. Why does the Fire need two buttons that bring you to the home screen?

  Whenever you tap it, Back brings you back to the last screen you were on, not just the home screen. If you open your Books library and then enter the Kindle Store and tap Back, for example, you're returned to your Library (hit Back again, and you're taken to the home screen).

- ▤ : Tap the Menu button to see options related to whichever section of the Fire you're in.

- 🔍 : Tapping the Search button allows you to search this section of your Fire for content.

Some apps are full-screen, so the options bar will not appear. In these cases, you can access the options bar by tapping the arrow at the bottom of the screen or by swiping your finger upward from the bottom of the screen (**Figure 1.52**).

Figure 1.52 *Tap the arrow icons at the bottom of the screen to access the options bar.*

Lock Screen

To lock your device to prevent errant taps from changing settings and other things, press the power button at the bottom of the Fire. This turns off the screen and locks your Fire.

Press the power button again to wake your Fire, and the lock screen is displayed (**Figure 1.53**). Here you'll see displayed in the background one of several lovely pictures Amazon commissioned especially for the Kindle Fire. The current time and date are also displayed, as well as an orange arrow pointing to the left. Swipe your finger along that arrow to the left, and your Kindle Fire unlocks.

Figure 1.53
Your Fire's lock screen displays the time and a lovely picture.

Accessing the Cloud

I've mentioned the cloud a few times already, and now it is time to explain what the heck it means. The *cloud* generally refers to services that host your data on computers maintained in a remote location (usually in a data center of some kind). You access this information via the Web, but they store it for you. Some cloud services you might be familiar with include Dropbox (*www.dropbox.com*) and Gmail (*http://mail.google.com*).

Amazon runs a host of cloud services of its own, and the Kindle Fire interfaces with many. Whenever you purchase digital music from Amazon's MP3 store, you have the option to store it in your Amazon Cloud Drive (*https://www.amazon.com/clouddrive/learnmore*), which in turn makes it available in the Amazon Cloud Player (*www.amazon.com/b?ie=UTF8&node=2658409011*). What's so cool about that? Well, any MP3s bought from Amazon are stored in its cloud for free and streamed to your Kindle Fire for free (you do need an Internet connection), effectively giving your Kindle Fire an unlimited capacity for music.

What about music you purchased from other places? Amazon allows you to upload up to 5GB of music for free. If that isn't enough, you can upload an unlimited amount for $20 a year (plus you get 20GB of additional space on your Amazon Cloud drive, which you can use to store any sort of documents you like). Amazon has created an MP3 Uploader to make it easier for you to upload your entire music collection to the Amazon cloud (**Figure 1.54** on the next page).

A few notes about the upload process, though: Music that has DRM on it (some music bought from iTunes, for example) cannot be uploaded to the Amazon Cloud Player (the uploader won't even allow you to select it). The only formats supported are MP3 (.mp3) and AAC (.aac), files must be

Figure 1.54

The Amazon MP3 Uploader allows you to upload music on your computer to Amazon's cloud.

less than 100MB in size, and uploading it to Amazon can take a long time if you have a large library (I uploaded about 17,000 songs over a 4-day period with my speedy FiOS connection).

Additionally, Amazon offers you unlimited cloud storage for all your Amazon-purchased digital items including books, music, and movies. The Fire allows you to either stream or download this content to the device so you can enjoy it on the go.

The Kindle Fire does have 8GB of built-in storage, though only about 6GB of that storage is available for your use (the other 2GB is taken up by files the Kindle Fire needs to operate). Amazon says that 6GB is enough space for about 80 apps and either 10 movies, 800 songs, or 6,000 books.

Keep in mind that only when you download apps, movies, and documents to your Fire do they take up some of that 6GB of space. Anything in the Amazon cloud, however, takes up no space on your Fire. That is why the Fire is designed to show you the content that you have on the cloud and download it only when you want to access it. (In other words, all your books are stored in the cloud, but when you tap one to open it, the book is downloaded to your device.)

Browsing with Silk and the Cloud

The Kindle Fire's browser, Silk, is connected to the cloud as well (**Figure 1.55**). Traditional browsers, like the one on your computer or smartphone, use the device's processor to render the page. This can be fairly computationally intensive depending on the page's complexity and could lead to the browser slowing down.

Figure 1.55
Silk displaying a website

This is especially vexing on mobile devices and tablets because battery power is a precious commodity. The more the processor has to work, the faster the battery will drain. Someone at Amazon thought, "Why not offload all that processor-heavy stuff onto our servers and then just deliver the page to the device?" That's what makes Silk different from other browsers: All your web requests go through Amazon's servers, which can decide what parts of the page will be handled on a server in Amazon's data center and which will be handled on the Fire.

note Any secure web requests (usually involving SSL, or Secure Sockets Layer), like those to your bank or other financial institutions, do not go through Amazon's servers. Those connections happen directly between your Fire and the institution's website so that Amazon won't be able to see any confidential information.

The end result of all this is that Silk performs faster and uses less battery life, which are both good things in my book.

In addition to speeding up your browsing by offloading complex operations to Amazon's servers, Amazon tracks usage on websites (anonymously). This sounds a little creepy I know, but this tracking is for a good purpose: intelligent prefetching of content. Imagine you're on the *New York Times* website. Many people access the *New York Times* using Silk, and Amazon's servers can take all that data and predict which link you're most likely to click. That page is then fetched just in case you click it (since most people do) while you're still looking at the front page. If you do, in fact, click that popular link, it'll load very quickly because it was already waiting for you.

While this cloud integration is very nifty and I'm sure Amazon will add even more features to Silk as time goes on, it does have some privacy concerns. Amazon states that it might cache (i.e., store) some information about your web browsing history for no longer than 30 days (generally). This data could include URLs, your IP address, and your MAC address, all of which could theoretically be used to identify you.

tip Check out the Amazon Silk Terms & Conditions to read Amazon's privacy information about Silk: *www.amazon.com/gp/help/customer/display.html/?nodeId=200775270*.

I'm quite comfortable with Amazon's privacy policy, so I happily take advantage of Silk's cloud component, but if you aren't as comfortable with this as I am, you can turn off the cloud acceleration feature of Silk entirely. When you're in the web browser, tap the Menu button in the options bar and tap Settings > Advanced > Accelerate page loading (**Figure 1.56**). Tap to uncheck, and now Silk will function like a plain old browser. Pages will take a little longer to load, but your web requests will be going straight to whatever websites you're visiting without first going through Amazon's servers.

Figure 1.56 *Turn off "Accelerate page loading" if you don't want your requests to go through Amazon's servers first.*

Managing Your Kindle Fire

Your Kindle Fire must be registered to an Amazon account in order to be really useful. This means that the registered account will incur all the costs whenever something from Amazon is purchased on that particular Fire. Eventually, you might want to give your Fire to someone else or just change the Amazon account registered on the Fire. If you need to go a step further, you can reset your Kindle Fire completely to factory settings, which wipes out all the content on the device as well as the settings.

Deregistering Your Fire

Deregistering your Fire retains all your settings and any content that has been downloaded to the device. Anything that the original Amazon account has stored on the Amazon cloud will not be accessible with the deregistered Fire. In fact, even though the content downloaded to the

Kindle Fire remains, when you register the Fire with a new account, you may not be able to open it. (In other words, Kindle books purchased with one account cannot be opened with another.)

To deregister your Kindle Fire, tap the Quick Settings icon in the status bar and then hit More > My Account (**Figure 1.57**). Tap the deregister link, tap OK in the warning, and now this Kindle Fire is no longer registered with that account (**Figure 1.58**).

Figure 1.57
*Deregister your
Fire before you
give it away.*

Figure 1.58
*This Fire is
unregistered.*

Enter the account information for the new account to which you'd like to register the Kindle Fire. Once that is all done, all the settings will carry over, and any personal documents, bookmarks, and the like will remain accessible to the new account.

You also deregister your Kindle Fire via Amazon's website using either your computer or Fire. The Manage Your Kindle website (*www.amazon. com/myk/*), which requires an Amazon account to log into, gives you control over a number of your Kindle-related settings. (All your Kindle devices can be managed here, not just the Fire.) Enter the username and password registered with your Kindle Fire, and your Kindle Library is displayed (**Figure 1.59**). What we're after is in the Your Kindle Account section.

Figure 1.59
The Manage Your Kindle website allows you to do a number of tasks.

Click or tap (depending on how you're accessing the site) the Manage Your Devices link to see a list of all the Kindles associated with the logged-in Amazon account (**Figure 1.60**). Each of the Kindles registered to this account is displayed in a list with the name of the Kindle, the Kindle e-mail address, any special-offer status, the type of Kindle, and a Deregister link.

Figure 1.60
All the Kindles registered to your Amazon account

Depending on how many Kindles you have registered with this account (I have seven Kindles actively registered with my Amazon account; I might also have a Kindle problem), you might have to scroll down to reach the Kindle Fire entry. Once you find the Kindle Fire's entry, click/tap Deregister.

A warning pops up telling you to deregister a Kindle only if you're giving it to another person (**Figure 1.61**). Click Deregister, and now your Kindle Fire will no longer be able to make purchases with your Amazon account.

Figure 1.61

A warning is displayed to make sure you know what you're doing.

tip You can also register your Kindle on this website, if you would rather not enter your username and password using the Kindle keyboard. Click/tap the Register a Kindle link at the top of the Kindle list. You'll need to have the Kindle's serial number in order to register via this method (**Figure 1.62**).

Figure 1.62

Registering a Kindle on the Manage Your Kindle site requires the Kindle's serial number.

You're probably thinking, "I suppose it is cool that I can deregister my Kindle Fire from Amazon.com, but why would I do that when it is so easy to do from the device itself?" If your Fire is stolen and you haven't set a lock screen password (see the "Securing Your Fire" section), you'll be very happy to have this functionality. You can deregister your Fire remotely, and the thieves won't be able to compound their theft by buying lots of stuff from Amazon (all on your dime). That'll show 'em!

Resetting to Factory Defaults

If you want to completely reset your Fire and erase everything on the device (including, but not limited to, personal documents, books, and music), you'll want to use Reset to Factory Defaults.

Tap the Quick Settings icon and then More > Device > Reset to Factory Defaults. Keep in mind that your Fire needs to have at least 40 percent of its charge, or else you won't be able to reset it (this battery level ensures that the Kindle Fire can erase itself and reset without losing power even if the power adapter isn't plugged in).

Once you tap Reset, a warning appears to keep you from accidentally resetting your Fire (**Figure 1.63**). Tap "Erase everything" (they are not kidding), and the Fire will restart itself. This process takes a few minutes, but once the Fire finishing rebooting, it is as if no one had ever used this Fire before.

Figure 1.63
Resetting to the factory defaults wipes all your content and settings off your Kindle.

Securing Your Fire

I'll admit it; I'm something of a security nut. I enable password protection on every device I own, and not even my wife knows what my passwords are (I told you, I'm a little nutty). The Fire ships without a lock screen password enabled, but I suggest you set one.

Setting a lock screen password does add a step to waking up your Kindle Fire. Instead of just swiping to unlock, you'll need to swipe and enter your password (which has to be at least four characters long) before you can interact with your Fire. The upshot to this extra step, though, is that anyone who picks up your Fire and swipes to wake it up will be asked for a password (stopping Fire thieves in their tracks) before they can access anything.

To enable a lock screen password, tap Quick Settings > More > Security (**Figure 1.64**). Here you'll find a number of security-related settings, but you want to tap Lock Screen Password. You're taken to a screen where you must enter your new password twice (**Figure 1.65**). Tap each field, and enter the same password in each. Your password, as I mentioned, must be at least four characters long, and it can be a mix of letters and numbers. Tap the Set button, and your Fire now has a password set.

Figure 1.64
A bunch of security settings are available; we're interested in Lock Screen Password here.

Figure 1.65
Enter the password you want to set twice.

When you wake your Fire from sleep and swipe to unlock it, you'll be greeted with one of two possible password screens. If you have set a password composed only of numbers, a number pad is presented for you to tap your password into (**Figure 1.66**). If your password is a combination of numbers and letters, a full keyboard appears for your password-typing pleasure.

Figure 1.66
If your password has only numbers, the lock screen displays a number pad.

Entering the correct password unlocks your Fire, which only makes sense. If you repeatedly enter an incorrect password (six times, to be exact), a message appears offering to reset your Kindle Fire since you seem to have forgotten your password (**Figure 1.67**). This serves dual purposes: If you do actually forget your Fire password, resetting the device will reset the password as well, and if someone other than you repeatedly tries to enter your password, at least they won't be able to use your Kindle Fire to purchase things on your tab.

Figure 1.67
Misentering your password six times prompts the Kindle Fire to offer to reset itself.

If you cannot remember the password for your Kindle, you can reset your Kindle to regain access.

Before doing this, please note that your Kindle will restart in a state similar to when it was new. This means the process will erase all data from your device, including your Amazon account.

You'll need to register your Kindle again before downloading items in your Amazon account.

| Do not reset | Ok reset |

note Changing your Kindle Fire's password requires you to enter the current password first.

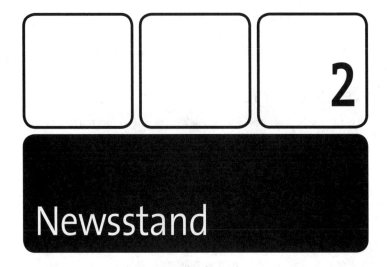

2

Newsstand

Newsstand is where all your Kindle magazine and newspaper subscriptions are gathered. Here you can read, subscribe to, and sample (with a trial subscription) a variety of newspapers and magazines right on your Kindle Fire. Traditionally, Kindle magazines and newspapers have been black-and-white affairs, because of the limits of the e-ink Kindles. The Kindle Fire, as you know, has a great color screen, and more than 400 magazines and newspapers now take advantage of this feature by offering their content in color. The subscriptions that offer only text-based reading experiences are called *text view* magazines, while magazines that offer a more printlike experience are called *page view* magazines. Subscriptions that support page view are labeled "Includes page view" in the Newsstand store both on the Kindle Fire and on Amazon.com.

In this chapter, I'll take you on a tour of the Newsstand on your Kindle Fire, show how to buy some magazines (both single issues and subscriptions), and lay out the different reading modes available to you.

Newsstand 101

To get to the Newsstand from the Fire's home screen, just tap Newsstand in the navigation bar (**Figure 2.1**). The first thing you'll notice is the shelf metaphor continues here. All of your current subscriptions (if you have any) and previously purchased single issues of Kindle magazines and newspapers are arranged on a series of shelves. Swipe up with a finger to scroll through the shelves if you have lots of magazines/newspapers. New issues of your current subscriptions will be delivered directly to your Kindle Fire and are denoted with a New icon (**Figure 2.2**).

Figure 2.1
The Newsstand library on your Kindle Fire lists all your periodicals.

Figure 2.2
When a new issue arrives, it sports this New banner.

Figure 2.3
Long tapping a magazine with back issues brings up a contextual menu.

If you subscribe to a magazine, chances are you'll have more than one issue in your archives; however, Newsstand seemingly displays only one magazine cover for each subscription. In Figure 2.1, you can see I have a subscription to the *New York Times Book Review*. If you look closely, you can see the icon is actually a stack of magazines; all the issues are represented by one icon. Long tap a magazine stack to bring up the contextual menu (**Figure 2.3**). Tap Show Back Issues to display all your issues of the selected magazine (**Figure 2.4**). Bring up the contextual menu again, and tap Hide Back Issues to restack them.

Figure 2.4
Now both the current and older issues are displayed on the shelf.

Before we jump into a magazine, let's check out the rest of this screen. At the top left you'll find the name of the content library you're currently in (Newsstand in this case), and next to that you'll find a way to toggle between content in the cloud or on your device. By default Newsstand shows you all of your subscriptions in the cloud. If you would rather see what magazines/newspapers you have on the device, just tap the Device toggle, and the list of locally stored subscriptions is displayed.

As with most of the other libraries on the Kindle Fire, the Cloud view is shown by default. Remember, this is content that you own, but it is stored on Amazon's servers. You need to download it before you can interact with it, which requires an active Internet connection. Any issues in the Device section have been previously downloaded and can be opened whenever you want regardless of the state of your network connection.

Rounding out the top section of the Newsstand is the link to the Newsstand store where you can purchase new subscriptions or single issues. I'll talk more about that in the section "The Store" later in this chapter.

Next up are your sort options for the library of content (the sort options are the same in both the Cloud view and the Device view): By Recent or By Title (shown in Figure 2.1). By default your subscriptions are displayed by the most recent issue, which makes sense since you're probably interested in reading the newest stuff. If you'd rather organize your subscriptions by title, you can just tap By Title, and the items are rearranged in alphabetical order.

At the bottom of the Newsstand screen is the standard options bar with the home icon, the back icon, the menu button, and Search. Tap the menu button to see the two view options that are available (**Figure 2.5**). The grid view, which displays the cover of each magazine and newspaper in a grid, is the default view. If you have lots of subscriptions, though, the grid can mean a lot of scrolling. List view compresses the view by just giving you a simple list with the name of the subscription and a small thumbnail (**Figure 2.6**). List view allows you to get more subscriptions onto the screen to save your fingers some work.

Figure 2.5
The options menu allows you to choose either grid or list view.

Figure 2.6
List view is more compact and informationally dense.

 Long tapping a magazine will allow you to add it to your Favorites on the home screen.

Reading

Newsstand offers two views for all its content: page view and text view. As mentioned at the beginning of this chapter, not all magazines and newspapers support page view, which replicates the printed artifact more closely, but text view is always supported. Tap a subscription or single issue in the Newsstand to start reading (if you are on the Cloud view, the issue will be downloaded to your device and then opened).

Once a magazine/newspaper opens, it is very easy to determine whether it supports page view. If the magazine looks much like the glossy version you would buy on an actual newsstand, with the complex layout and images, then it is one of the 400+ that have been created to take advantage of the Kindle Fire's screen (**Figure 2.7**). On the other hand, if you are presented with a table of contents that looks like a list of links to the articles in the issue, this magazine/newspaper hasn't been optimized for the Kindle Fire (**Figure 2.8**); however, you can still read it on your Fire.

Figure 2.7
A magazine that supports page view looks just like its printed counterpart.

Figure 2.8
Magazines that support only text view display a table of contents when you open them.

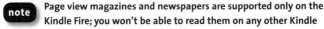

note Page view magazines and newspapers are supported only on the Kindle Fire; you won't be able to read them on any other Kindle devices. Text view is supported across the Kindle family.

Page View

As you can see in Figure 2.7, some magazines on the Kindle Fire look very much like their physical counterparts, without the bothersome threat of paper cuts looming over you. These magazines are displayed in page view. Turning the page is as easy as tapping either side of the screen (left to go one page back, right to go one page forward). You can also swipe left and right to turn the page, if you prefer.

A full page of a magazine on a 7-inch screen can be a little tough to read, but you can zoom in to increase the size of the text or check out a particular detail in a photo. Pinch your fingers at the point you would like to zoom into, and as your fingers slide against the Fire's screen, the magazine content zooms in so you can read it (**Figure 2.9**). To zoom out, you can double tap any point on the screen, or you can pinch outward to see the whole page.

Figure 2.9
Pinch or double tap to zoom in on a page.

Figure 2.10

The page view navigation uses thumbnails of the magazine's pages so you can quickly see which page you want to jump to.

Tap in the middle of the screen to bring up the navigation (**Figure 2.10**). The navigation consists of page thumbnails of the whole magazine with page numbers indicated below each. You can scroll through these thumbnails by swiping left and right. You can also use the slider beneath the thumbnails to quickly scrub through the magazine's contents. Once you've found a page you'd like to read, tap the thumbnail, and it is displayed.

When you tap the middle of the screen, a few other things appear in addition to the navigation: the status bar, some information about the magazine you're reading, the view toggle, and the options bar at the bottom of the screen. The top left of the screen displays the name and date of the magazine you're currently reading and on the top right are two buttons that allow you to toggle between page view (the default) and text view (more on this in the next section) (**Figure 2.11**).

Figure 2.11

The page view and text view buttons allow you to switch back and forth between the two views.

Figure 2.12
The options bar in a magazine

The options bar has the usual suspects and a couple of new additions: the home button, the back button, the Text icon (displayed in page view, this will be covered in the next section), the Contents icon, and Search (**Figure 2.12**).

Figure 2.13
Tapping the Contents icon brings up a nice table of contents so you can quickly jump from article to article.

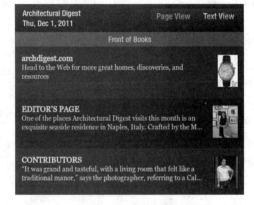

Tap the Contents icon to display a table of contents (**Figure 2.13**). Scroll up and down with your finger to see all the article titles; when you find one you're interested in, tap it, and it is displayed (this works the same way in text view).

Changing Orientation

When you're reading a print magazine, you're generally seeing two pages side by side. People who design magazines take this as a given when laying out articles and advertisements, but you may have noticed in all the screenshots of page view that only one page is displayed at a time. That's because when your Kindle Fire is held in portrait orientation (taller than it is wide), only one page is displayed. When you turn your Kindle Fire on its side, the orientation changes to landscape, and two pages now appear at once (**Figure 2.14**).

Pinching to zoom in to read the text works in landscape just as well in portrait orientation.

Figure 2.14
Putting your Fire in landscape mode allows you to see two pages of a magazine at once.

Text View

Text view is supported by all periodicals on the Kindle store and across all Kindles: It is the lowest common denominator (**Figure 2.15**). In fact, page view–capable magazines can also be displayed in text view by tapping the text view button at the upper right of the screen (visible after you tap the middle of the screen).

Figure 2.15
Text view pulls out the text and pictures from the magazine and presents them in a simple way.

note You can't switch to text view when you're looking at a full-page advertisement in page view. Just turn the page, and text view is enabled once more.

Text view presents just the text of the articles on your Kindle's screen. The great thing about text view is that it uses the entire screen, so there's no need to pinch to zoom in and out to read the text. The downside is that all that fancy layout and design is no longer visible (or doesn't exist if you're reading a text view–only periodical).

Tap the middle of the screen to bring up the options bar, and you'll see that the Text icon is now tappable. Tap it to change the text size, line spacing, margins, and color mode (**Figure 2.16**). As you tap each option, the screen automatically changes so you can easily decide whether you like the changes.

Figure 2.16
Text view allows you to change font size, line spacing, and more.

You can even change the font that is used by tapping Typeface in the Text options and selecting one from the list (**Figure 2.17**).

Figure 2.17
While in text view, you can also set what typeface is used, using this list.

Searching

Search is supported both within individual issues in Newsstand and on the Newsstand home screen. These two searches give very different results, though, because of the scope of their searches.

When you're on the Newsstand home screen, tap into the Search box and start typing a search query. The search results are limited to your magazine and newspaper titles. This search is, in effect, a filter for your subscriptions. Looking for a particular magazine in your large Newsstand library? Search for it here, and it'll show up in the results with the name of the magazine and a thumbnail of the cover (**Figure 2.18**).

Figure 2.18

Searching your Newsstand library for a particular magazine using Search

Search works differently when you're in an issue of a magazine or newspaper. Tap the middle of the screen to bring up the options bar and then tap the Search icon. Enter your search term and tap Go. The entire magazine/newspaper is searched for the term you entered, and all the locations are displayed in the search results grouped by section, with the search term highlighted in yellow (**Figure 2.19**). Tap the item you're interested in reading, and it is displayed for you.

Figure 2.19

Searching within a magazine. Your search term is highlighted in yellow when it is found in the text.

Tap the back button in the options bar to exit the in-magazine search results.

The Store

Now that you know how to read and search things in the Newsstand, it is time to add some content to your library. One great thing about subscriptions for the Kindle Fire is that each magazine and newspaper offers a free trial ranging from a couple of weeks to 90 days (this is a special offer that is limited to a small group of magazines). You can try the magazines for a while, and if you don't like them, feel free to cancel (I'll show you how to do that later in this chapter).

You can purchase subscriptions and individual issues either directly on your Kindle Fire or via Amazon.com (and have the content automatically appear on your Fire). I'll show you how to do both.

Kindle Fire

Tap the Store button at the top right of the Newsstand on your Kindle Fire to browse the offerings (**Figure 2.20**). The top of the Newsstand store features a Search box and a Library button. Below that is a special section that highlights certain magazines that the Amazon editors choose (in Figure 2.20, the 17 magazines featuring 90-day trials for Kindle Fire owners are presented).

Below the featured section are different groupings of magazines. Scroll down with your finger to see all the groups.

To the right of these groups are the sections of the Newsstand store that you can browse: Magazines and Newspapers. Tap either one to see a list of categories (**Figure 2.21**). Tap the categories to see the full list of items in the category.

Figure 2.20
The Kindle Fire's Newsstand store

Figure 2.21
All the categories of magazines available in the store

You can also get to this list view by tapping one of the "See all" links (shown in Figure 2.20) on any of the groups of magazines (**Figure 2.22**). The name of the group is displayed in orange at the top with the number of magazines included in the results along with the current sorting. The results themselves consist of the cover of the most recent issue, the name of the magazine, its page view compatibility, and the price per subscription duration (monthly or weekly).

Figure 2.22
A list of the featured magazines. All searches and lists in the Newsstand store have the same layout.

Tap the Refine button to change how the results are sorted and to filter by category and customer reviews (**Figure 2.23**). Your sort options include Bestselling (the default), Price: Low to High, Price: High to Low, Average Customer Review, and Publication Date. Tap the one you would like to use, and it is applied to the results list.

Figure 2.23
You can refine any of the lists by tapping the Refine button and selecting from the options.

note When you search the Newsstand using the Search field at the top of the screen, the results screen is just like the one shown in Figure 2.22, and the options available by tapping the Refine button are also the same.

Tap one of the magazine covers to see more information about it (**Figure 2.24**). Details about the magazine are displayed to the right of the current issue's cover. These details include the magazine's name, publisher, and "Includes page view" if the selected magazine supports page view (if this isn't listed, then only text view will be available). Frequency of delivery is listed (monthly, weekly, and so on) below, as is the monthly price (i.e., the price when you subscribe) and the price of the current issue (which is generally more expensive).

Figure 2.24
The Smithsonian *magazine's entry in the Newsstand store allows you to buy the current issue or subscribe.*

Directly below the information about the magazine are two buttons: an orange Subscribe Now button and a gray Buy Current Issue (with the date of the current issue displayed underneath).

When you tap the subscription button, the current issue of the magazine starts to download to your device, and you'll automatically receive the latest magazine on your Kindle Fire when it is available (**Figure 2.25**). Keep in mind that every magazine/newspaper available for the Kindle Fire includes a trial period in which you get some issues for free, but at the end of the trial (usually 2 weeks, but some offer 90-day trials), you're charged the subscription fee.

Figure 2.25
Tap Subscribe or Buy Current Issue, and the last issue will be downloaded to your Fire.

Your 14-day free trial has started.

Downloading... View Order Summary

Purchased by accident? Cancel Order

tip To conserve space, only the seven most recent issues of a subscription are kept on your Kindle. When a new issue is released and you already have seven issues of that magazine on your Fire, the oldest is deleted. If you want to make sure a particular issue isn't deleted, long tap it and tap Keep in the contextual menu.

Buying the current issue charges your Amazon account and downloads the issue to your device.

Finally, the last section of information about the magazine/newspaper includes a description, customer reviews, and product details (such as the publisher). There's also a link to the item's page on Amazon.com.

note You'll notice some magazines in the Newsstand store display an icon instead of the most recent cover. These magazines are actually apps, which are installed in the Apps section of your Kindle Fire.

Menu Button

At the bottom of the Newsstand store you'll find the standard buttons: home, back, forward, and menu. Tapping the menu button reveals four buttons: Storefront, Magazines, Newspapers, and Kindle Account (**Figure 2.26**).

Figure 2.26
The options menu allows you to jump from one section of the store to another.

The Storefront button takes you to the Newsstand storefront page no matter which screen you're on. The Magazines and Newspapers buttons take you to the full list of each of those types of periodicals available for your Fire.

Tapping Kindle Account takes you out of the Newsstand store and opens the Manage Your Kindle website in Silk (Fire's browser). You'll learn more about this in the "Canceling Subscriptions" section.

Amazon.com

You can to subscribe to magazines and newspapers or buy single issues for your Fire on Amazon.com from your computer.

Open Amazon.com in your browser of choice, and navigate to the Kindle Newsstand section (**Figure 2.27** on the next page). All the magazines and newspapers available on the Kindle Fire's store are available here as well.

 Blogs are listed in the Amazon.com Newsstand as subscriptions, but the Fire doesn't support this functionality.

Figure 2.27
The Kindle Newsstand on Amazon.com

When you find a magazine you want to subscribe to, click it (**Figure 2.28**). The cover is displayed, along with some information about the magazine in a bulleted list. One of the bullet items for magazines that support page view is "Available only on Kindle Fire."

Figure 2.28
A magazine's entry in the Amazon.com Kindle Newsstand

You can either buy a subscription by clicking the "Subscribe now with 1-Click" button or buy the current issue by clicking the "Buy now with 1-Click" button displayed under the subscription button.

Either way, you have to let Amazon know where to deliver this magazine to by selecting your Kindle Fire's name from the "Deliver to" menu.

For Kindle Fire–only magazines, the "Deliver to" option defaults to the Kindle Fire.

Canceling Subscriptions

Now that you've subscribed to a bunch of magazines and newspapers, taking advantage of the trial period, you probably would like to know how to cancel a subscription. This functionality isn't built into the Kindle Fire Newsstand store; you must go to the Manage Your Kindle website in order to cancel a subscription.

Point your browser of choice to *www.amazon.com/myk* and enter the Amazon account details that are registered to your Kindle Fire. After you log in, you can do a wealth of things here, from canceling subscriptions to directly downloading previously purchased Kindle content.

Under Your Kindle Account in the left navigation, click or tap "Subscription settings" to see all your current Kindle subscriptions and modify them (**Figure 2.29**). All your subscriptions along with the billing info, where they are being delivered, and an action menu are displayed in the Subscription Settings section.

Figure 2.29

The Subscription Settings allow you to cancel your subscriptions individually.

Click the Action menu and select "Cancel subscription." A confirmation message appears asking you to select a reason for the cancellation (**Figure 2.30** on the next page). Select your reason or add your own, and click or tap the yellow Cancel Subscription button. You will no longer receive this magazine, and an e-mail to that effect is sent to your inbox as confirmation.

Figure 2.30
When you cancel a subscription, Amazon wants to know why.

note You can always read the magazines/newspapers you already own, even after you cancel your subscription.

Privacy Settings

Do you ever wonder why magazines and newspapers offer subscriptions for so much less than the cover price? It is because in exchange for a deeply discounted rate on their content, you're giving the magazine/ newspapers something very valuable: your contact and demographic information. They use this not only to sell advertising for their magazines but also as a way to target market their readers.

Amazon, by default, shares your name and address with the publisher of any Kindle periodical you purchase. If you aren't thrilled with this, you can change the setting.

Go to the Subscription Settings of the Manage Your Kindle site (see the previous section for instructions on how to find this page and log in). Scroll down until you see the section Privacy Preferences for Newspapers and Magazine Subscriptions. This lists all your subscriptions, past and present, and what information (e-mail or mailing address) has been shared with the publisher (**Figure 2.31**).

Privacy Preferences for Newspapers and Magazine Subscriptions			
Choose which information is shared with publishers for marketing purposes. Learn more about Privacy			
Title	E-mail address	Use name and billing address for marketing purposes	
Architectural Digest	Not Shared	Yes	Edit
Fantasy & Science Fiction, Free Exclusive Digest	Not Shared	No	Edit
The New York Times Book Review	Not Shared	Yes	Edit

Figure 2.31 *Your privacy settings determine whether Amazon shares information about you with the publishers of magazines you subscribe to (by default it does).*

Click the Edit link on the far right on the magazine/newspaper privacy setting you want to change in order to see the Privacy Settings section (**Figure 2.32**). You can uncheck both your name/billing address and e-mail so that nothing is shared, or you can do any combination of the two. You can even share an e-mail address other than the one you use with Amazon.

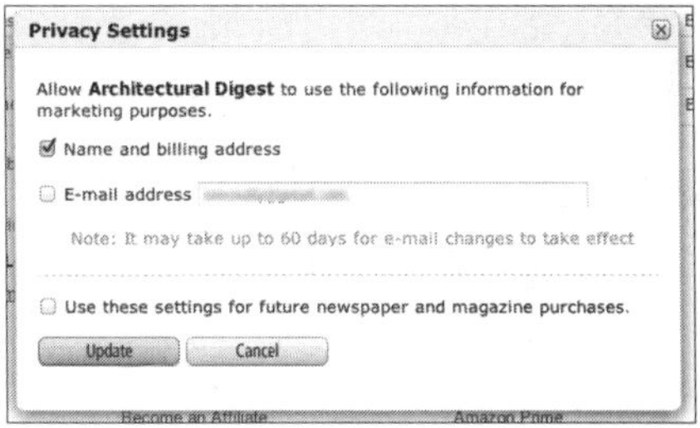

Figure 2.32 *When you change an individual privacy setting, you can check a box to make these settings the default for future purchases.*

Privacy Settings   ⊠

Allow **Architectural Digest** to use the following information for marketing purposes.

☑ Name and billing address

☐ E-mail address

   Note: It may take up to 60 days for e-mail changes to take effect

☐ Use these settings for future newspaper and magazine purchases.

   Update   Cancel

If you want to apply this same settings no matter which periodical you're purchasing, make sure to check the "Use these settings for future newspaper and magazine purchases" option.

Click the yellow Update button, and your privacy settings have been changed.

Books

The Kindle has built its reputation on having a great book-reading experience. The Kindle Fire continues this tradition, while adding a host of additional functionality.

This chapter covers reading, purchasing, and managing your Kindle books.

Books Library

Tap Books on the Fire home screen to access your book library. By default the books on your device are displayed lined up on virtual shelves. Tap Cloud at the top of the screen, and all your Kindle books, both those on the device and those stored on Amazon's servers, are displayed (**Figure 3.1**). You can tell the books apart because the ones that haven't yet been downloaded to your Fire have an arrow icon at the bottom right of the cover.

Figure 3.1
*The book library
on your Kindle
Fire displays all
your Kindle books.*

No matter which section of your library you're looking at, Cloud or Device, you have the same three sort options: By Author, By Recent, and By Title. Tap the one you would like to use, and the books rearrange in that order (by default your most recently purchased books are displayed first).

Swipe up with your finger to scroll through all the books on either list.

At the bottom of the screen you'll find the options bar with the home, back, menu, and search buttons. Tapping the menu button lets you switch the view from grid to list (**Figure 3.2**).

Figure 3.2
Grid and list views are available by tapping the menu icon in the options bar.

List view displays all your books as a list (shocking, I know) and gives you a little more information at a glance (**Figure 3.3**). On the left is the book's cover with the name of the book, the author, and the book's status. A book can have a few different statuses:

Figure 3.3
You can sort your library by author, recent, or title.

- *Not downloaded*: This book is on the cloud but hasn't been downloaded to the device. The download icon is displayed here.
- *New*: Newly downloaded books will display a New icon New here.
- *Partially read*: If you've read some of the book, your progress is displayed here as a percentage of the amount read.

Tap the search button to search your library. You can search by author or title (the actual text of the book will not be searched).

Reading

Tap a book that you would like to read in either your Cloud or Device library. If the book isn't on your device, it will be downloaded and then opened; otherwise, the book opens to either the first page or the last page you were on thanks to WhisperSync (more about this in a moment).

Turning "pages" on the Fire is easy: To advance a page, either tap the right side of the screen or swipe to the left (to go back a page, do the opposite).

Figure 3.4

Tap the center of the screen while reading a book to see the options bar and the bookmark ribbon.

While you're reading, you can add notes, highlights, and bookmarks to the book, which get synced to the cloud via WhisperSync. WhisperSync is a free Amazon service that wirelessly syncs all sorts of data from your Kindle books to Amazon's servers. Whenever you open a book on another Kindle device or app, all of these additions are available to you thanks to WhisperSync.

 WhisperSync requires an active Internet connection to function.

Tap the center of the screen to bring up the options bar, as well as the bookmark icon in the upper-right corner of the page (**Figure 3.4**). Tap the bookmark icon to save your current location (**Figure 3.5**).

Figure 3.5
Tap the bookmark ribbon to bookmark a page.

Tap the screen again to hide the options bar (which we'll revisit shortly), and long tap your finger on a word in the book. The selected is high-lighted in blue, and the word's definition appears along with a menu (**Figure 3.6**).

Figure 3.6
A word's definition appears when you tap it, along with a couple of other options.

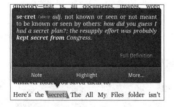

If you want to see the full definition of the selected word, tap Full Definition. This will take you out of the book you're reading and load the New Oxford American Dictionary (included with your Fire). Once you're finished with the definition, tap in the center of the screen and tap the back button in the options bar to return to the book you were reading.

Figure 3.7
Adding a note using the on-screen keyboard

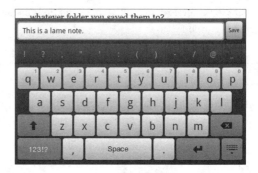

Under the definition are a couple of buttons: Note, Highlight, and More.... Tap Note, and a text field and keyboard appear at the bottom of the screen (**Figure 3.7**). Type in your text note and tap the Save button when you're finished. A tiny note icon appears next to your selection indicating that a note is available (**Figure 3.8**). Tap it, and a pop-up with the note text appears along with the location of the note, as well as edit, delete, and close buttons (**Figure 3.9**).

Figure 3.8
This blue icon means a note has been left in this location.

Figure 3.9
Tap the note icon to read the text of the note. You can edit or delete the note from here as well.

To select more than one word, first long tap a word. That word will be selected, and a little magnifying field appears showing you the words under your finger. While still pressing against the screen, move your finger along the words you'd like to highlight. You can also move your finger down to highlight entire lines of text (**Figure 3.10**). To expand your selection, tap and drag on the little blue handles at either end of the selection.

Note
Highlight
More...
But aren't all those files flung across your Mac? How do they show up in this folder while they're also in whatever folder you saved them to?

Figure 3.10
Selecting more than one word allows you to highlight entire passages.

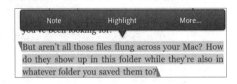

The same menu appears with the highlight option. Tap the highlight, and the selected text is highlighted in yellow (**Figure 3.11**).

But aren't all those files flung across your Mac? How do they show up in this folder while they're also in whatever folder you saved them to?

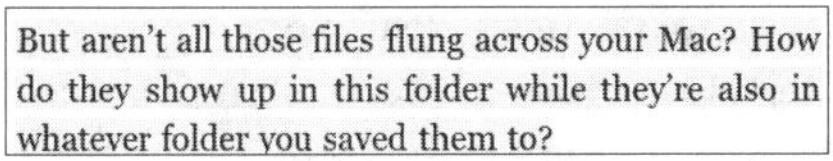

Figure 3.11
Highlighting shows up in yellow.

To delete a highlight, long tap any word in the selection and tap Delete Highlight. Highlighting will be removed from the entire selection.

Tap the More... button to see three addition actions (**Figure 3.12**):

Search in Book
Search Wikipedia
Search Google

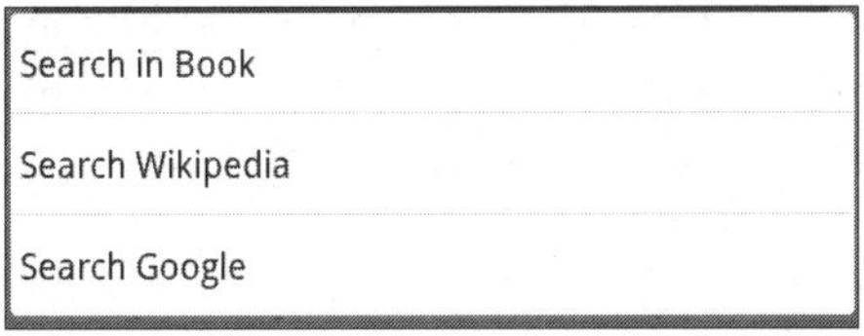

Figure 3.12
Tapping the More button reveals three search options.

- *Search in Book*: This searches the full text of the book for whatever word or phrase you selected (**Figure 3.13**). The search term is highlighted in the results, which are grouped by chapter. You can also search inside the book by tapping the search button in the options bar of any book.

Figure 3.13
When you search within a book, the search term is highlighted. Tap a location to display it.

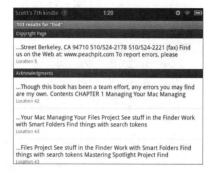

- *Search Wikipedia*: Tap this to search *http://wikipedia.com* for the selected text. To get back to your book, tap the menu icon and tap the Back to Reading button (**Figure 3.14**).

Figure 3.14
Tap the menu icon to reveal the Back to Reading button.

- *Search Google*: This functions just like Search Wikipedia, except that it performs a Google search using the selected words as the search term.

Navigation

You have more options for navigating your Kindle books than just going back and forth one screen at a time. Tap the middle of the screen to bring up the options bar. Above the options bar your current location is displayed, along with the percentage of the book you've read and a slider (**Figure 3.15**). To quickly go to location in your book, just move the slider. The location number will change, and when you take your finger off the screen, the location you selected will be displayed.

Figure 3.15
The location bar allows you to quickly scrub to a new location.

Location 199 of 3683 • 5%

Locations

I know what you're thinking at this point, what the heck are locations? Locations are sort of like page numbers, except they are far more granular. Each word in a Kindle book has a specific location in the book, designated with a number. This number is a *location* in Kindle speak.

Amazon has introduced "real page numbers" for Kindle books, which map the page numbering from a printed edition of a book to the Kindle version. At the moment, real page numbers aren't supported on the Kindle Fire, but I think that will be addressed in a software update in the not too distant future.

Tap the menu icon in the options bar to bring up some important navigation (**Figure 3.16** on the next page).

Figure 3.16

Tapping the content icon brings up several locations that you can jump to by tapping, including any notes, bookmarks, and highlights you've made.

The top section of the navigation options lists a few options:

- *Cover*: Tap this to see the cover of the Kindle book.

- *Table of Contents*: The table of contents is just like the table of contents for any other book, only better. Each part of the table of contents is a link, and when you tap it, you're taken directly to that section. A physical book can't do that!

  While you're in the body of a book, you might come across some blue underlined text that looks suspiciously like a hyperlink (or just a link, as the kids say these days). Those are, in fact, links to either other locations in the book (like the table of contents) or a website. Tap it just like you would any other link, and you're taken to that location/site.

- *Beginning*: No matter where you are in the book, you can hop right to the start of the book by tapping Beginning.

- *Location...*: If you have a location number, tap this, and then you can enter the number and jump right to it (**Figure 3.17**).

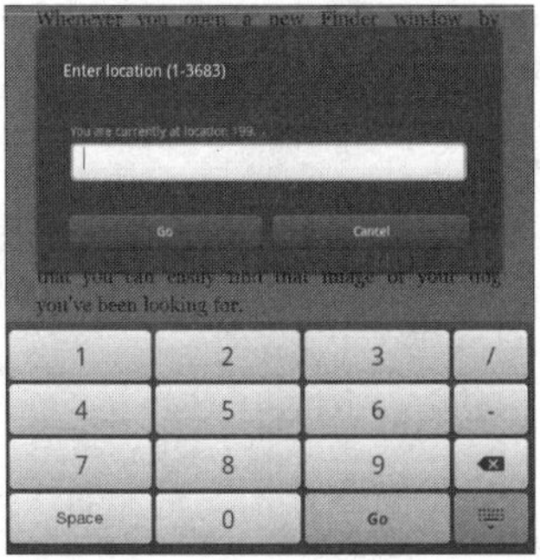

Figure 3.17
Enter a location and then tap Go to jump to the exact location in your book.

- *Sync to Furthest Page*: WhisperSync stores your current location, notes, bookmarks and highlights in Amazon's cloud. Usually this syncing happens automatically, but sometimes it needs a little nudge. Sync to Furthest Page is that nudge.

The final section in the navigation is My Notes and Marks (shown in Figure 3.16). All of your notes, bookmarks, and highlights for this book are listed here. You can read the full text of your notes and the entire phrase that you've highlighted right from here.

Swipe up with your finger to scroll through the list, and tap an entry to go to that location in the book. If you long tap, a menu appears with two options: View and Delete (**Figure 3.18**).

Figure 3.18
Long tapping a note, bookmark, or highlight allows you to view or delete it.

Appearance

I love physical books, but despite the great pleasure I take in reading them, holding them, and even smelling them, they do have some issues. As I am aging (seemingly more rapidly than ever), my eyes aren't what they used to be. Sadly, a physical book doesn't care. It was typeset with a particular font, font size, and margins, and that's the way it is.

Kindle books, on the other hand, allow you much greater control over how the text actually looks on your screen.

To see your text options, tap the middle of the screen and then tap the text button in the options bar (**Figure 3.19**). The text options are broken up into two groups just like those that are available when you're reading a magazine in text view (see Chapter 2 for more details).

Figure 3.19
The Font Style options allow you to change the font size, among other things.

Font Style lets you set the font size from eight choices, set the line spacing and margins out of three options, and set the color of the background and text.

Just tap each option, and the change is applied.

Typeface gives you a list of fonts you can choose for your book.

 These changes are global, so they will impact how all of your books are displayed on the Kindle Fire.

Store

Tap the Store button at the top right of the book library to buy some books from Amazon. The store looks very much like the Newsstand store (**Figure 3.20**). It works pretty much the same way, too.

Figure 3.20
The Kindle Store on the Fire

Various groupings of books are shown, with recommendations based on your purchase history at the top. Swipe with your finger to see all the recommended books. Tap the See All button at the top right of each grouping to see all the books listed.

At the right of the screen you'll see a listing of the various sections of the Kindle Store: Books, Kindle Singles, Kindle Newsstand, Editor's Picks, Kindle Owners' Lending Library, NY Times Best Sellers, and Children's Picture Books. Tapping a section either brings up a list of categories within that section of the store that you can then see a list of books from or takes you directly to the section.

At the top you'll see a search field that you can use to search for your favorite author or a book title. Tap the field, type your query, and tap Go. The search results return with the book cover, title, author, star rating, and price in a list (**Figure 3.21**). Tap the Refine button to further refine your search results. You can change the sorting method, limit which categories of books you want to include, and filter based on average customer review.

Figure 3.21

A search in the Kindle Store shows the cover of the book, title, author, rating, and price.

note All of the results in the store, whether they are search-generated or a list of books, use the Refine button in the same way.

Tap a book to see its details page that lists a description, print length, similar items, customer reviews (you might have to swipe up with a finger to see the reviews), product details (like sales rank), and a link to the title's entry on Amazon.com (**Figure 3.22**).

What will be of most interest are the two buttons near the top of the screen. One is labeled "Buy for…" with the price of the book, and the other is Try a Sample.

Figure 3.22
A book's entry in the Kindle Store. Tap the orange button to buy the book.

When you tap Try a Sample, a small sample of the book is added to your book library, and the button turns green (**Figure 3.23**). Tap it to read the sample. When you get to the end of the sample, you have the option to purchase the full book by tapping the Buy Now link or tapping the "See details..." link to return to that book's entry on the Kindle Store (**Figure 3.24**).

Figure 3.23 *After you tap the Try a Sample button and the download is complete, it turns into a green "Read sample now" button.*

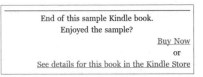

End of this sample Kindle book.
Enjoyed the sample?

Buy Now
or
See details for this book in the Kindle Store

Figure 3.24 *At the end of a sample are two links: a Buy Now link and a link to the book's entry page.*

note Samples are denoted with a small icon in your library (**Figure 3.25**).

Figure 3.25
A sample is labeled in your book library.

The Kindle Store options bar includes a menu icon. Tap it to reveal some shortcuts to parts of the store (**Figure 3.26**). Storefront will take you back to the storefront no matter what screen you're on, Books will take you to the books section, Kindle Singles (short e-books about a variety of topics written just for the Kindle store) takes you to that section, and Kindle Account actually takes you to the Manage Your Kindle section of Amazon.com.

Figure 3.26
The menu options in the Kindle Store let you jump to different sections with a tap.

Children's Books

The Kindle Fire has some tricks up its sleeves just for children's books. The e-ink Kindles aren't the best way to read kid's books since they so often feature great color pictures that would be rendered in black and gray. Not so much fun.

The Kindle Fire, however, has a great color screen, which is why there is a whole section of the Kindle Store devoted to Fire-optimized children's picture books. Some of these books feature Kindle Text Pop-Up, which expands the text on the page and makes it very easy to read.

Tap the Children's Picture Books button on the right side of the screen in the Kindle Store to see the list of available books. The description of the book will tell you whether it features Kindle Text Pop-Up or not (**Figure 3.27**). Purchase the book as you normally would.

Figure 3.27
This children's book supports the Kindle Text Pop-Up technology.

Open the book, and you'll see that it features large pictures and relatively little text. Some these books won't allow you to change orientation when you're reading them because the pictures are so big they fit only in landscape mode. Double tap some text, and it will pop it up for easier reading (note that the Text button in the options bar doesn't offer you any controls over the fonts for these particular books) (**Figure 3.28**).

Figure 3.28
Kindle Text Pop-Up in action

Graphic Novels

Graphic novels are sort of like picture books for adults in that they feature lots of artwork. Most graphic novels, though, also include a lot of text to move the story along. Some of that text can be hard to read, especially since you can't pinch to zoom when reading a graphic novel on the Fire (I assume this limitation will be addressed in a software update).

However, if you double tap a panel, Kindle Panel Preview kicks into effect. The panel zooms out so you can read the entire panel (**Figure 3.29**). Tap the right of the screen to go to the next panel. You can read the entire comic panel by panel so you won't miss a word of dialogue. Double tapping again brings you to the standard full-page view.

Figure 3.29
Kindle Panel Preview lets you read a graphic novel panel by panel.

tip To find graphic novels in the Kindle Store, tap the Books section and select Comics & Graphic Novels from the categories list.

Kindle Owners' Lending Library

The Kindle Owners' Lending Library is available only to Kindle owners who also happen to be Amazon Prime members (remember, a free one-month Prime trial is included with your Kindle Fire) (**Figure 3.30**). Just like it sounds, you can borrow Kindle books from a selection available in the Kindle Owners' Lending Library at no additional cost. As you can see in Figure 3.30, any book in the lending program has a Borrow for Free button. Tap that button, and the book is downloaded to your device and added to your library. The borrowed book looks just like any other book in your Lending Library.

Figure 3.30

A book in the Kindle Owners' Lending Library. Tap Borrow to download the book to your Fire.

To return a borrowed book, log into Manage Your Kindle (*www.amazon.com/myk/*) and select "Return this book" from the Action menu (**Figure 3.31**).

Figure 3.31

To return a borrowed book, click the "Return this book" link available in the Manage Your Kindle site.

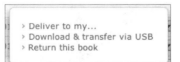

Although you can borrow only one book a month from the Lending Library, you have as long as you need to read the book. Take your sweet time, but keep in mind that you can borrow only one book at a time.

The Kindle Owners' Lending Library is available only on hardware Kindles; the Kindle applications are not supported.

tip Many public libraries allow you to borrow books using your Kindle. Check this website to see whether your local library supports Kindle lending: *http://search.overdrive.com/*.

From Amazon.com

If you're away from your Kindle Fire but you have a hankering to buy a book, you can do it right from Amazon.com and send it to your Kindle Fire. Find the Kindle book you want to buy in the Kindle Books section of Amazon.com.

Select your Kindle from the "Deliver to" drop-down either in the green "Buy now with 1-Click" box or in the "Try it free" box (**Figure 3.32**). Then click either the orange 1-Click button or the "Send sample now" button. When next you turn on your Fire and it is connected to the Internet, the book will be available in your library.

Figure 3.32
Select which Kindle you want your Amazon.com book order to.

One thing to note is that no matter which Kindle you send your purchased Kindle books to, they will appear in the Cloud section of the Books library. Samples, however, are available only on the Kindle they were either requested from or delivered to.

Downloading Books When You Don't Have a Wi-Fi Connection

The only network connection your Kindle Fire has is a Wi-Fi connection. This is great when you're in range of a Wi-Fi network, but what if there's no Wi-Fi around? If you have a wired connection for your computer but no wireless connection, you can still get new books onto your Fire.

You can download books from Amazon.com to your computer and then transfer them to your Fire via a mini-USB cable (not included with the Fire).

Point your browser to Manage Your Kindle (*www.amazon.com/myk/*) and log in with your Amazon username and password. By default Your Kindle Library is displayed, listing all your Kindle books (Figure 3.33). Next to each Kindle book you'll find an Action button. Click the Action button for the book you want to download and select Download & Transfer via USB.

Figure 3.33

The Your Kindle Library section on Manage Your Kindle

(continues on next page)

Downloading Books When You Don't Have a Wi-Fi Connection (continued)

From here you select which Kindle you are going to transfer the file to from the drop-down and then click Download (**Figure 3.34**). Select a location on your computer to save it.

Figure 3.34
"Download and transfer via USB" allows you to get new books onto your Fire even when it doesn't have a Wi-Fi connection.

Now the book is on your computer, but you need to get it onto your Kindle Fire. Connect your Kindle Fire to a USB port on your computer using a mini-USB to USB cable. The Kindle will go into USB mode and appear on your computer (either on your Desktop on a Mac or in File Explorer on Windows).

Double-click the Kindle icon on your computer. This is the Kindle's file system, but no need to worry about it. Just drag the book file you downloaded into the Book folder. Disconnect the Fire from your computer, and the book now appears in your on-device book library.

Music

Given that the Kindle Fire has a relatively low amount of onboard memory (about 6GB), you might be tempted to think that it isn't a great music device. Most of us have rather large digital music collections (I have something like 18,000 tracks stored on 86GB of hard drive space on my computer), and only a tiny chunk of a large collection can fit on a Fire. Although that is true of on-device storage, let's not forget about the cloud. You can use Amazon's cloud services to give your Fire an unlimited capacity for music (as long as you have an Internet connection).

This chapter will cover the music interface and all the ways to get music onto your Fire, as well as what to do with it when it is there.

Getting to Your Music

Tap Music on the navigation bar to enter the Music library on the Fire
(**Figure 4.1**). At the top you'll see the top navigation of the Music library:
Music, your two libraries (Cloud/Device), and a Store button.

Figure 4.1

*The Kindle Fire
Music Cloud
library*

By default, your Cloud library is displayed. Tap Device to see your local
library, though if you don't have any music stored on your Kindle Fire,
you'll see an alert telling you that there isn't any music on your device
and why not tap the big orange button to buy some from Amazon?
(**Figure 4.2**). Tapping the "Shop the Music store" button takes you to the
Fire music store (more on that in a bit).

When you have music in either of your libraries, the interface is identical
despite that the music is stored in different places.

Figure 4.2
If your on-device library is empty, Amazon suggests you buy some music.

 **note** Don't forget that you must have an Internet connection to listen to any music from your Cloud library. Music in your Device library can be listened to whether or not you're connected to the Internet.

Under the main navigation are the four different sections of your music library:

- *Playlists*: Playlists on your Fire are just like playlists on every other media player. They are lists of songs you create. The neat thing, though, is when you create a playlist in your Cloud library, it is available in the Amazon Cloud Player for the Web.

- *Artists*: This is a scrolling list of all the artists in your Music library along with the number of albums and songs from that artist.

- *Albums*: This is a scrolling list of your albums with the album cover to the left, the name of the album in white text, and the number of songs on the album.

- *Songs*: The final section of your Music library is Songs, the basic building block of any Music library. This list, much like the Albums list, shows the album cover, the name of the song, the artist, and one additional piece of information: the song's duration.

Your music is also searchable. Just tap the search button in the options bar, and the Search box appears. You cannot search across all your music in both libraries, Cloud and Device, at once. If you want to search both libraries, you'll have to search one and then the other.

Each section of the Music library (Playlists, Artists, Albums, and Songs) has its own search results format. If you search the Albums section, albums are returned with album cover art. If you search for artists, the artists and the number of albums and songs you have belonging to them are returned.

Playlists

You can create a new playlist right on your Fire. Tap Playlists > Create new playlist. Type in your playlist's name in the "Create new playlist" pop-up and tap Save (**Figure 4.3**). Next add some music to your playlist by scrolling through your songs and tapping the plus button next to the songs you want to add (**Figure 4.4**).

Figure 4.3
Name your new playlist something that makes sense given what songs you plan on adding to it.

Figure 4.4
Tap the plus icon to add songs to your playlist.

This isn't the most efficient method of looking for particular songs. Tap the Search box at the top of the Add Songs to Playlist screen and type the name of a song, artist, or album. The results will be displayed, and you can tap the plus sign to add songs to your playlist.

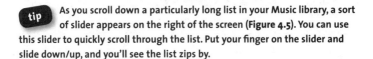

tip As you scroll down a particularly long list in your Music library, a sort of slider appears on the right of the screen (**Figure 4.5**). You can use this slider to quickly scroll through the list. Put your finger on the slider and slide down/up, and you'll see the list zips by.

Figure 4.5
This little tab appears while you're scrolling. Press your finger against it, and you'll scroll through a long list in no time.

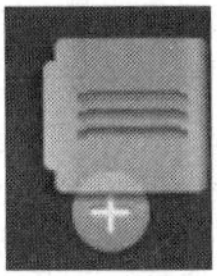

Tap the Done button, and your Fire displays an "Updating playlist" message as it creates your playlist (**Figure 4.6**). Once the playlist is created, it is displayed so you can either play the songs or edit it by tapping the Edit button to add/remove songs.

Figure 4.6
Tap Done, and the playlist is saved.

Now that you have a new playlist, you can do some cool things to it. In the playlist list, long tap a playlist, and the contextual menu appears with some options (**Figure 4.7**):

Figure 4.7
The playlist's contextual menu allows you to download it to your device, among other things.

- *Download playlist*: If you know you won't have Wi-Fi access but you really want to listen to some of your sweet playlists, you can download the playlist, and all the songs that it contains, to your device. This option appears only on playlists in the Cloud library.

- *Add more songs to playlist*: I just covered how to create a playlist. If you have an existing playlist and want to add more songs to it, tap this option, and you'll be taken to the Add Songs screen (shown in Figure 4.4).

- *Rename playlist*: Not happy with the name of your playlist? You can change it by tapping this option, typing a new name, and then saving it.

- *Delete playlist from Cloud Drive or device*: Want to great rid of the playlist? Tap this and the playlist is gone, but the music on the playlist is still in your Music library.

tip When you play songs from a playlist, the playlist appears on the home screen's Carousel. Long tap the playlist's icon to add it to your Favorites. This trick works for the special playlists as well.

Special Playlists

You can delete or modify all the playlists you create on your Fire, but there are some playlists that are automatically generated. In your Cloud library you'll see two playlists that allow you to download only the songs they contain; you can't rename them or delete them. Latest Purchases and Latest Uploads list exactly what you think they do, but here's the clever part: You don't add songs to them manually but rather by your actions.

When you upload songs to your Amazon Cloud Player (more on this in the "Adding Music to Your Fire" section), they are added to the Latest Uploads list automatically. When you purchase songs/albums from the Amazon MP3 store (either on the device or via Amazon. com) and add them to your Cloud Drive, they appear on the Latest Purchases playlist.

The Device library contains one special playlist, Latest Additions, which lists all the songs/albums recently added to the device.

Playing Music

Now that you know how to get around your Music library, it is time to play some music (if you don't have any music available in either your Cloud or Device library, check the "Adding Music to Your Fire" section to find out how to get your tunes loaded).

No matter what section of your library you're in (Playlists, Artists, Albums, or Songs), playing some music is easy. Tap the playlist, artist, album, or song you want to play. Once it is done loading, the song starts playing

(**Figure 4.8**). The Now Playing screen is shown with a big image of the album art, if available, displayed. Above the album art some information is displayed, from left to right:

Figure 4.8

The Now Playing screen displays the album art of the currently playing song, as well as the playback controls.

- *A number x of y*: This designates the song's position in the currently playing playlist where x is its position and y is the total number of songs on the playlist. Obviously, when you're playing a song from a playlist, y will be the number of songs on the playlist. When you're playing an album, it'll be the total number of tracks on the album. Interestingly, when you just play a random song from your library by tapping it from the Songs list, this number is still displayed. That's because your Fire queues up to 2,000 songs when you play a particular song. This queue allows the Fire to prefetch the next song on the list, which is particularly useful when you're playing from your Cloud library. Prefetching the song ensures you have a smooth streaming experience.

If you have fewer than 2,000 songs in your library, y will display your total number of songs.

- *Song Scroll*: Next you'll see the name of the song displayed in large white type with the album and artist displayed underneath. If one part of this information doesn't fit into the allotted space, it'll scroll so you can read the whole thing.

- *List view*: Tapping this icon will bring you to a list of all the songs on either the Now Playing queue, the playlist you're playing, or the rest of the songs on the album you're enjoying. You can tap any song on this list to play it instead of whatever is currently playing.

Beneath the album art is a slider showing how long you've been listening to the song, your current position, and how much time is left. You can scrub the track by pressing your finger on the slide control and sliding back and forward.

Directly under that slider are some familiar play controls:

- *Shuffle*: Tap this icon to shuffle the songs and play them random order; tap again to play the playlist/album/queue in order. When active, this icon turns orange.

- *Play controls*: The Back, Play, and Forward buttons are so ubiquitous that you certainly know what to do with them.

- *Repeat*: If you want to repeat the entire contents of a playlist/album/ queue, tap this icon once. Tapping it twice will repeat the currently playing song over and over again (something I like to do on occasion) (**Figure 4.9**). Tap again to stop repeating.

Figure 4.9 *The repeat button can be used to repeat a playlist or a single song over and over again.*

Finally, there is a volume slider that you can use to turn the music up, though keep in mind that just like the volume slider in the Quick Settings (Gear icon), it controls the system volume of your Fire, so everything will be louder, not just your music.

 When you turn your Fire on its side, the play controls are displayed in landscape mode.

When you long tap the album art of the currently playing song, a contextual menu appears with a number of choices (**Figure 4.10**):

Figure 4.10
Long tapping the currently playing song brings up this contextual menu.

- *Clear Now Playing Queue*: Tap this to clear all the songs from the queue. This will force your Fire to re-create the queue and play songs in a new randomized order (if you have shuffle on).

- *Download song*: Available only when you're playing a song from your Cloud library, this will download the song to your Fire.

- *Remove from Now Playing*: If you don't want the song to be in the Now Playing queue, tap this button. When you hit the previous button, the song you remove won't play, but rather the song that played before it will.

- *View album*: View all the tracks on the currently playing song's album.

- *View artist*: View everything by the currently playing song's artist.

- *Shop artist in store*: Want to see what else the singer/group of this track has for sale? Tap this, and a search for the artist will take place in the Fire Music store.

tip You can also clear the Now Playing queue by tapping the options menu and then tapping "Clear queue."

As a song is playing, you can leave the Now Playing screen, and the music will continue to play. Tap the Library button to go back to exploring your Music library, or tap the Store button to shop for some new music. As long as you are in the Music section, a mini-player appears at the bottom of the screen displaying the currently playing track and play controls (**Figure 4.11**). You should be aware of some playback settings. Tap the menu icon in the options bar and then Settings (**Figure 4.12**). You're interested in the Playback Settings section, which includes three items: Lock-screen controls, Enable equalizer modes, and Equalizer Mode.

Figure 4.11
Mini playback controls appear at the bottom of the Music library when a song is playing.

Figure 4.12
Playback settings accessible from the menu icon in the options bar

Selecting "Lock-screen controls" allows you to pause, skip, and change the volume of the currently playing track right from the lock screen (**Figure 4.13**). When enabled (by tapping the checkbox), you'll be able to access the controls in Figure 4.13 when you unlock your Fire and a song is playing.

Figure 4.13
With lock-screen controls enabled, you can control your music without having to navigate to the Music library.

This is great if you want to change the song and then lock your Fire again. If you want to actually unlock your Fire to use it, tap the Unlock icon in the upper-right corner of the Now Playing window. This does add an extra step to unlocking when a song is playing, so be sure to keep that in mind when enabling lock-screen controls (tap to clear the checkbox and disable lock-screen controls).

An equalizer tweaks the sound coming from your Fire to better re-create the "actual" sound of music. By default equalizer modes are disabled, but you can enable them by tapping "Enable equalizer modes." The Equalizer Mode list then becomes available. Tap it to see the full list of equalizers you can apply to your music (**Figure 4.14**). Tap one to apply it, but keep in mind that this is a global setting. The mode will be applied to all the music you play here. You can always change it to another mode, if you like, but per-song/album equalizer settings are not available.

Figure 4.14
Equalizer mode offers up a number of equalizers to tweak the sound of music playback.

Adding Music to Your Fire

You can add music to your Fire in three ways: upload it from your computer to your Amazon Cloud Drive by using the Amazon Cloud Player, transfer it to your Fire using the Fire's USB mode, or buy it from the MP3 store on the Fire.

This section discusses each method.

Cloud Drive

I mentioned Amazon's Cloud Drive and Cloud Player in the first chapter of this book because they are both important to the Fire. Here's a refresher: Amazon gives anyone with an Amazon account (that's you) 5GB of free storage space on its servers. You can store whatever you like using this storage: documents, music, or videos. Once you've uploaded your files to your Cloud Drive, you're able to access them with a web interface. In addition, Amazon will store any music you buy from the Amazon MP3 store in your Cloud Drive for free. This music doesn't take up any of the storage space, so you will still have 5GB of storage even if you purchase 8GB of music from Amazon. For more information about Cloud Drive, check out *https://www.amazon.com/clouddrive/learnmore*.

Amazon Cloud Player allows you to play all those songs stored on your Cloud Drive on a variety of devices through your web browser (*www. amazon.com/cloudplayer*), on an Android-powered smartphone, and on the Kindle Fire. This is where all the music in the Cloud library on your Fire comes from.

To automatically add any music you buy from Amazon (on either your Kindle or Amazon.com's MP3 store) to your Music library, tap the menu icon in the options bar and select Settings. There is a whole section called Amazon Cloud Drive Settings (**Figure 4.15**). Tap "Delivery preference" to set either "Save purchases to your Cloud Drive" or "Save purchases to this device." I suggest making use of the free Amazon Cloud Drive storage to save the storage space on your Fire.

Figure 4.15
Amazon Cloud Drive settings allow you to save all your Amazon MP3 purchases to the cloud.

If you want to have your cake and eat it too, tap "Automatic downloads" to have the music saved to your Cloud Drive automatically downloaded to your Fire.

note Your Kindle Fire has only 6GB of space that you can use to store things. To check how much of that you're using, tap Quick Settings (the gear icon) > More > Device. The amount of available storage is the first thing displayed.

Uploading Your Own Music to Your Cloud Drive

Now that your Amazon purchases are saved to your Cloud Drive, why not upload all the music on your computer to your Cloud Drive? This way, you can access all your music from your Kindle Fire without taking up any space on the device (assuming you have an active Wi-Fi connection).

Music files (only non-DRMed MP3s and AACs can be uploaded to your Cloud Drive) from sources other than Amazon do count toward your storage limit, so you can upload only 5GB for free. However, for $20 a year Amazon allows you to upload an unlimited number of music files and adds 20GB to your Cloud Drive, bringing your total available storage for other files to 25GB.

No matter which plan you decide to go with, uploading your music to your Cloud Drive works the same way. On the computer with the music you want to upload, point a browser to Amazon.com and then click MP3s & Cloud Player (**Figure 4.16**). Click Cloud Player for the Web, and a new window will open (**Figure 4.17**).

Figure 4.16 *Click MP3s & Cloud Player to launch your Cloud Player from Amazon.com.*

Figure 4.17 *Amazon Cloud Player for the Web*

You'll find a yellow Upload button with the amount of space you have left on your Cloud Drive for music storage (**Figure 4.18**). Click it, and you'll be prompted to install the Amazon MP3 Uploader. Follow the directions to install the application on your computer (PCs and Macs are both supported).

Figure 4.18
Click the "Upload your music" button to launch, or download, the Amazon MP3 Uploader.

Once it is installed, it will launch automatically and start searching your computer for music (**Figure 4.19**). It searches only well-known locations (the default location for your iTunes library and the Music folder on your Windows computer). If you store your music in a custom location, the Uploader won't be able to find it, but it will allow you to manually select a folder. Select the folder you store your music in and click Scan, and the Uploader will merrily scan that folder for supported music files.

Figure 4.19
The Amazon MP3 Uploader scanning a computer for music

When the scan is completed, a window appears telling you how many files you can upload to Amazon and how many you've previously uploaded (the Uploader is smart enough to upload only those files that weren't there when it last ran) (**Figure 4.20**).

Figure 4.20
Success. The Uploader has found 27 new songs to upload.

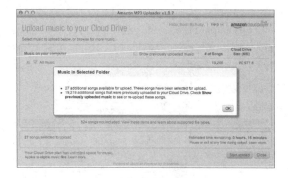

Click OK, and now you're ready to upload these files. All the files that you can upload to your Cloud Drive will be displayed. You can uncheck any files, playlists, or folders you don't want to upload. Once you're happy with your selections, click the "Start upload" button, and the upload commences (**Figure 4.21**). Depending on how many files you're uploading and the speed of your Internet connection, this process can take quite a long time. An estimated time is displayed, as is a progress bar for each upload.

Figure 4.21
The Uploader lists all the music it has found along with a link to view the songs that it cannot upload.

Chances are your Music library will have some songs that the Uploader won't upload. In Figure 4.21, you can see a yellow alert at the bottom of the screen that says "524 songs not included." Click the link to see the full list of incompatible files and why they couldn't be uploaded (**Figure 4.22**). You can copy the list to the clipboard so you can paste it into a text document for future reference.

Figure 4.22

Music that can't be uploaded for one reason or another. Click the Copy to Clipboard button if you want to save this list.

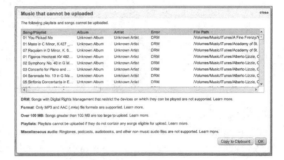

Downloading from the Cloud
=======

Sometimes you won't have Internet access, which means all those songs in the cloud won't be accessible. For times like this, you can download songs from your Cloud Drive to your Fire ahead of time. Just look for the orange download icon on every cloud song, album, artist, and playlist (**Figure 4.23**). When you tap the icon, it will download all the tracks associated with whatever content you were viewing: all the songs on a selected playlist, all the songs and albums from a particular artist, or just a specific album or song.

Tap the options bar and then Downloads to track the progress of the download.

Figure 4.23

Tapping the download button will download the song, playlist, or album to your Fire.

As the files upload, they will be added to the Latest Uploads playlist on your Kindle Fire (and in the Cloud Player for the Web) so you can listen to them right away.

Transfer Your Own Music

If you're more of a do-it-yourselfer, you can load your Kindle Fire with music directly. Keep in mind that any music added to your Fire via this method will use up space on the device.

You'll need a micro-USB cable to do this. Plug your Fire into a USB port on the computer with the music files on it using a micro-USB cable. The Fire will go into USB drive mode and show up either on the Desktop of your Mac or in the Windows File Explorer as a drive called Kindle (**Figure 4.24**).

Figure 4.24
When you connect your Fire to your computer, it becomes a USB drive called KINDLE.

Double-click the drive, and you'll see all the directories on your Kindle (**Figure 4.25** on the next page). Notice there is a Music folder; that's where you're going to add your music. The Fire will play back MP3s and AACs; no other audio files are supported, though. If you move other types of files into the Music folder, they will take up space; they just won't be playable.

Figure 4.25
These are all the directories on your Kindle Fire.

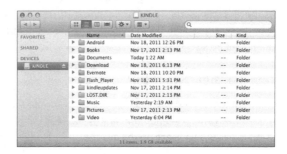

Drag and drop files, or whole directories, of music onto the Fire's Music directory. When you're finished transferring songs, tap the Disconnect button on the Fire's screen, and your songs will appear in the Device Music library.

Buying Music on the Fire

Tap the Store button to shop in the Amazon MP3 store right from your Fire (**Figure 4.26**). This store is much like the other stores on the Kindle. At the top you'll find Featured albums you can swipe through. Below that are some other sections of the store: Bestsellers, New Releases, and Genres. Tap any of those buttons to be taken to that section of the store.

Figure 4.26
The Kindle MP3 store

Rounding out the storefront are some recommendations for you based on your Amazon purchase history. Both Albums and Songs are listed; toggle between the two lists by tapping the appropriate button. Each album or song has a button with the price displayed next to it.

Tap an album to see a list of all the songs on the album, along with individual prices for each track (**Figure 4.27**). Tapping one of the tracks starts a 30- or 60-second sample so you can get a taste for what you're about to buy.

Figure 4.27
Tap the play icon to preview a song for 30 seconds, and tap the orange button to buy it.

If you like what you hear, tap the button with the price. It turns into a green Buy button. Tap again, and depending on your settings, the songs are added to your Cloud Drive, downloaded to your Fire, or both (**Figure 4.28**).

Figure 4.28
When you purchase a song or album, it can be added to your Cloud Drive, your Fire, or both.

You can listen to the songs as soon as the process is complete.

If you aren't sure what exactly you want from the MP3 store, you can always search. The search results include Albums and Songs buttons, so you can switch between the two (**Figure 4.29**). Tapping an album from the search results gives you more details about it, and tapping a song plays the preview.

Figure 4.29
Searching for music in the store is very easy.

5

Video

The Fire's screen just begs you to watch video on it. Luckily, there is an entire library devoted to your video content, both streaming and on the device. This chapter will cover watching video on your Fire, including streaming Prime videos for free, purchasing and downloading videos from Amazon.com, and transferring your own videos to your Fire.

When you enter the Video library on your Fire by tapping Video from the home screen, you'll notice something right off the bat: You're in the Video store, not your Video library (**Figure 5.1** on the next page). Unlike every other section of the Kindle Fire, the Video section shows you the store by default. You can see your library, which includes all the shows/movies you're purchased from Amazon, by tapping the Library button at the top of the screen.

Figure 5.1

Unlike other content areas, the Video section of your Fire opens to the Video store.

Video Store

As I mentioned, when you enter the Video section, you're thrown right into the Video store. The store is broken up into three sections (shown in Figure 5.1): Prime Instant Videos, Movies, and TV Shows. Prime Instant Videos include TV shows and movies that are available to Amazon Prime members to stream for free on their Fires (and other supported devices), while the other sections list movies and shows that are available for renting/purchasing.

Prime Instant Videos

Tap "View all" in Prime Instant Videos to see a list of the available content in this section (**Figure 5.2**). By default you're in the Movie section; you can get to the TV section by tapping the TV button at the right of the screen. Both sections are a list of scrollable movie/TV show posters.

Figure 5.2
Prime Instant Videos are free to stream for Amazon Prime members.

Prime Instant Video Movies

The Popular Movies tab is listed first, but you can switch to other sections with a tap. To switch to another list of Instant Videos, just tap one of the buttons above the movie posters. Swipe with your finger to see additional buttons in the section navigation. Once you've found a movie you're interested in watching, tap it to see some details (**Figure 5.3**). To the right of the movie poster, details are displayed including the movie name, star ranking, and MPAA rating. A Watch Now button rounds out that section of the movie entry (the Prime logo lets you know this movie is part of Instant Video).

Figure 5.3

A movie's entry in the Video store lets you tap a button to start streaming.

If you want to see a trailer for the film, tap the Watch Trailer button (this button won't appear if a trailer isn't). The trailer plays once you tap the button.

Right next to the Watch Trailer button is the Purchase Options button. Streaming Prime Instant Video movies is free, which works well when you have a Wi-Fi connection. When you are without an Internet connection, you can't stream movies. That's why you can also purchase or rent movies for viewing. Tap the Purchase Options to see your options for this particular movie (**Figure 5.4**).

Figure 5.4
Most Prime videos have additional rental/ purchase options.

The Rental & Purchase Details button brings up a window explaining the differences between renting a movie. You have 30 days to watch a rented movie; once you start watching it within those 30 days, you have a 24- or 48-hour period (depending on the rental) to finish watching the movie. After that period, if you want to watch the movie again, you'll have to rent it again or stream it.

A synopsis of the movie appears under the poster, and some more details about the movie including the main actors, director, and run time are listed. Rounding out the screen are some movies/TV shows that people who bought the movie you're viewing also bought. Swipe to see the whole list, and tap one to be taken to its detail page.

To watch a Prime Instant Video, just tap the Watch Now button, and as long as you have an Internet connection, the video player will launch and prepare your video for viewing (**Figure 5.5** on the next page).

Figure 5.5
The loading screen that is displayed as Amazon prepares for your video

Prime Instant Video TV Shows

Tap the TV button to see all the shows that are available for streaming on Prime Instant Video, with the popular TV shows listed by default (**Figure 5.6**). Much like the Movies section, tap another section to see other groups of TV shows.

Figure 5.6
The Prime Instant Video selection of TV shows

Tap a poster of a show you want to watch, and you'll see that there are some differences between movies and TV shows on the Video store (**Figure 5.7**). The biggest difference is that TV shows have multiple seasons and episodes within those seasons. Underneath the show art and synopsis you'll find the season bar. Each available season has a button on the bar (swipe to access additional seasons that might not fit on the screen). Tap a season to see all the episodes within that season and the ways you can watch it.

Figure 5.7
TV shows have multiple seasons, which, in turn, contain multiple episodes.

Each episode will list the Prime price ($0.00 if it is available on Prime Instant Video) and the rental price.

Since each episode of a show usually contains some unique details about the plot and actors, it stands to reason that they would each have their own details page. Tap an episode to see more details and the play options (**Figure 5.8** on the next page). Much like the movie detail page, there is a Watch Now button, a Watch Trailer button, and a Purchase Options button, all of which function identically to their movie counterparts. The More Episodes button will bring you back to the full list of episodes in the season.

Tap the Watch Now button, grab a beverage, and sit back and relax while you watch an episode of a TV show on your Fire.

Figure 5.8

The details of a particular episode of "Deep Space Nine"

Renting and Purchasing

Tapping the View All button on the other two sections of the video store, Movies and TV, takes you to a screen almost identical to the list of Prime Instant Videos (**Figure 5.9**). What makes this screen different? Well, I neglected to point something out to you in the Instant Videos section (aren't I a clever writer?): At the top of any of the movies/TV shows listings, you'll see a toggle between Prime and All. When you tap Prime, only movies available in Prime Instant Videos are displayed; when All is tapped, all the movies/TV shows that Amazon has for rent/sale are listed in addition to Prime Instant Videos.

Tapping a poster for a movie/TV show available for purchase/rent shows the same details as those listed for Prime Instant Videos. Two orange buttons are the only difference: One shows the price for a rental, and the

Figure 5.9
All the movies and TV shows available for rent and purchase on the Kindle Video store.

other is labeled "See all" (**Figure 5.10**). Tap the "See all" button, and a pop-up appears listing the different options for rental or purchase (**Figure 5.11**).

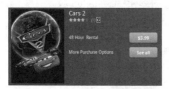

Figure 5.10 Cars *isn't available in Prime Instant Streaming, but you can rent it or purchase it.*

Figure 5.11 *Renting is much cheaper than buying a movie, as you would expect.*

  As a rule of thumb, renting a movie or show will cost much less than purchasing it.

Some shows and movies are available for rental and purchase in HD, but the Fire can't actually play HD video. When you try to purchase/rent an HD video, a warning appears telling you that you can go ahead and rent this video in HD, but it will play back only in standard definition on your Fire (though you can watch it on another device that supports HD if you want) (**Figure 5.12**).

Figure 5.12

You can rent, and purchase, HD movies on the Fire, but the Fire can't play HD video. This warning lets you know that if you watch the video on your Fire, it'll be in SD.

When you're ready to rent a movie/show, just tap the button with the price. It'll change to a green Rent button. Tap it again, and your Fire talks to Amazon for a few seconds. Once the rental goes through, a green banner appears at the top of the details page displaying when your rental expires (**Figure 5.13**). Two other buttons also appear: Watch Now and Download.

Figure 5.13

After you rent a movie or show, you can download or stream it.

Tapping Watch Now allows you to watch the movie/show via streaming. If you are renting this movie/show because you're going on a trip away from Wi-Fi, you should download the video to your Fire.

Tap the Download button, and your rental starts (**Figure 5.14**). Keep in mind that you can download a rental to only one device (your Fire in this case), but you can always stream it from the Web or another compatible device.

Figure 5.14
Downloading the video starts the 48-hour rental period.

Tap "Start rental," and the movie/show starts to download.

Library

Tap the Library button to see your Video library (**Figure 5.15**). Keep in mind that the Video library contains only those videos that you've purchased/rented from Amazon.com. Much like the other libraries on your Fire, the Video library has Cloud and Device libraries. Both libraries are further divided into Movies and TV shows. You can sort the contents of your library By Recent or By Name.

Figure 5.15
The Video library displays all your purchased Amazon.com videos.

When you tap a movie/show that is in your Device library, you can, of course, watch the video, and you can delete it from your device by tapping the Delete button. Next to the Delete button, the duration of the movie is displayed along with the size of the movie file (**Figure 5.16**).

Figure 5.16
A green banner lets you know that you own this video, and you can delete it from the device.

Tapping movies/TV shows in the Cloud library will display the detail screen for the video. You can either download the video to your device or tap the Watch Now button to stream it from the cloud.

Watching a Video

Now that you've found something you want to watch, just tap the Watch Now button. An Amazon Video logo appears as the video is buffered. Video plays back only in landscape mode; the screen will not automatically rotate.

The video playback controls should be familiar to anyone who has used a video playback mechanism of any sort in the last 20 years or so (**Figure 5.17**). The volume slider is in the upper-right corner of the screen. Slide it up and down to increase/decrease the volume. At the bottom of the screen is the Play/Pause button as well as the duration slider. On the left end of the slider is the time elapsed, and on the far right the time remaining in the video is displayed. If you're streaming the video, the progress bar serves double duty. As the video is buffered to your device, the progress bar fills with a white bar. You can skip to any point in the video by tapping the bar or by sliding the control. Finally, on the upper-left corner is a button that lets you rewind in 10-second increments. Tap it 3 times to rewind 30 seconds (the more taps, the further back you go).

Figure 5.17
The video controls are displayed here.

While you're watching a video, the controls fade out, so the entire screen is devoted to what you're watching. Tap the screen to bring the controls up, including the options bar that you can use to tap either the home or back button to exit the video.

If you leave the video partway, WhisperSync notes where you left off. When you resume watching the video, whether on your Fire or another supported device, you can either start from where you left off or start from the beginning.

Playing Your Own Videos

It is possible to load up your Fire with a bunch of your own movie files, but keep in mind that the Kindle Fire supports a limited number of video types: MP4 and VP8. VP8 is a very new video format, and you probably don't have any videos using it, which means MP4 is the way to go in general.

Once you're sure that the video you want to transfer to your Fire is in a compatible format, you are ready to transfer it from your computer to your Fire using a micro-USB cable. Connect the Fire to your computer using the cable. Swipe to unlock your Fire, and it will go into USB mode.

Now you should have a drive called Kindle on your computer. Double-click it, and drag your video, or videos, into the Video folder.

Once the transfer completes, your videos are now sitting on your Fire. To watch the video you just transferred, you might be tempted to go to your on Device Video library. If you do that, you'll notice the video you added isn't listed there. That's because the Video library on your Fire contains only Amazon-purchased or rented videos.

Where did your video go? It is on your Fire, worry not; you just need to use the Gallery app to view it. Tap the home button to go to your Fire's home screen, and then tap Apps. Find the Gallery app and tap it (**Figure 5.18**). If you haven't downloaded the app yet, tapping it will automatically download it to your Kindle.

Figure 5.18
To watch your own videos, you need to launch the Gallery app.

Once the Gallery app launches, you'll see there is a video (or videos, depending on how many you transferred) waiting for you (**Figure 5.19**). Tap the Video icon to open the video gallery, and then tap the video you transferred to watch it. The same playback controls are available here as in the Video library.

Figure 5.19
Tap the Videos section to watch your transferred video.

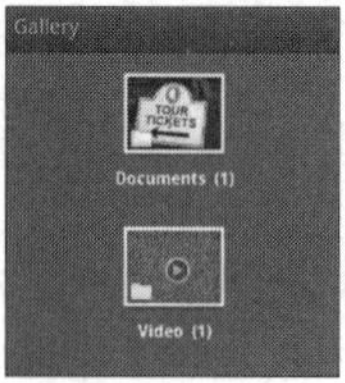

Docs

We all have more documents in our lives than we know what to do with: Word files, PDFs, and more. Wouldn't it be great if you could just e-mail them to your Kindle and have them waiting for you on the device? Well, you can! The Docs library on your Fire is dedicated to storing your personal documents, as long as they are in a supported format.

You can get your documents onto your Fire in one of two ways: using the Kindle Personal Documents Service or transferring them using a mini-USB cable. This chapter will cover both methods.

Kindle Personal Documents Service

The Kindle Personal Documents Service is pretty neat. Your Kindle is assigned a unique e-mail address to which you can e-mail documents. These documents are sent off to the Kindle Personal Documents Service, registered with your account, converted to a Kindle Fire native format (if needed), and wirelessly delivered to the Docs library on your Kindle.

When you transfer documents this way, you gain a couple of benefits: Your personal document is added to your Amazon Cloud drive (just like a purchased Kindle book) so you can access them from the Archive folder of any e-ink Kindle (or another Fire registered to your account). Any notes, bookmarks, or highlights you make in your personal document are synced across Kindles. And, of course, your location in the personal document is also synced across devices.

Before I get into how to do this, I'll talk file formats. The Kindle Personal Documents Service works only with a certain set of file formats, though it does cover some popular file types. You can use this method to transfer the following file types to your Fire:

- Word documents (.doc/.docx)
- HTML (.html/.htm)
- Rich text (.rtf)
- A variety of graphics files (.jpeg, .jpg, .gif, .png, .bmp)
- Kindle format e-books (.mobi, .azw)
- PDFs (.pdf)

The Setup

Now that you know the types of files supported, how do you actually use this magical service? Your Fire has a unique e-mail address assigned to it. Simply attach one of the files from the previous list to an e-mail addressed to your Fire's e-mail address and hit Send. That's it!

However, in an effort to avoid having random people filling your Fire with personal document spam (wouldn't that be horrible?), you set approved e-mails that are allowed to send documents to your various Kindle addresses (all Kindles get assigned an e-mail address, not just Fires).

To add your e-mail address to the Approved Personal Documents Service's e-mail list, log into the Manage Your Kindle site (*www.amazon.com/myk*) with your Amazon account. Click Personal Document Settings in the Your Kindle Account section (**Figure 6.1**).

Figure 6.1

The Personal Document Settings section on Manage Your Kindle determines who can e-mail things to your Kindles.

There is a wealth of knowledge about your Amazon Personal Documents settings here. You can even change the e-mail address for particular Kindles to something you'll better remember. (In the Send-to-Kindle E-Mail settings section, click Edit next to the Kindle you want to assign a new e-mail address, enter the new address, and click Update.)

At the moment, you just want to add an e-mail address to the approved sender list, so scroll down until you see a section called Approved Personal Document E-mail List (**Figure 6.2** on the next page). Any e-mail address listed here can send personal documents to any of your Kindles, including your Fire.

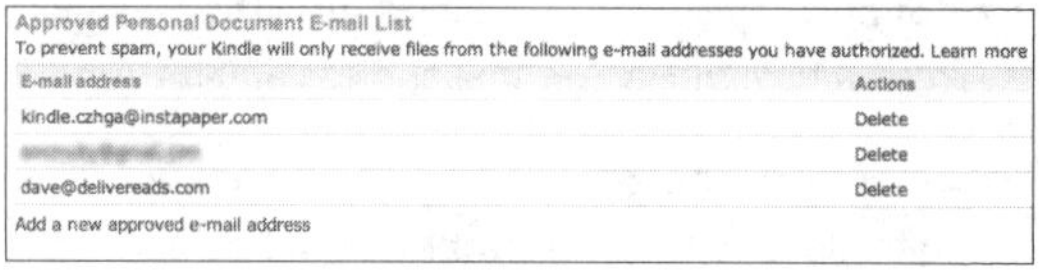

Figure 6.2

*Only e-mail
addresses on
the Approved
Personal
Document E-mail
List can send
documents to
your Kindle Fire.*

Approved Personal Document E-mail List	
To prevent spam, your Kindle will only receive files from the following e-mail addresses you have authorized. Learn more	
E-mail address	Actions
kindle.czhga@instapaper.com	Delete
	Delete
dave@delivereads.com	Delete
Add a new approved e-mail address	

Adding a new e-mail address, or your first one, is simple. Click the "Add
a new approved e-mail address" link. The "Add a new approved e-mail
address" form pops open (**Figure 6.3**). Fill in an e-mail address, or if you
want to allow everyone from a particular organization to send to your
Kindle, enter the last part of the e-mail address (@organization.org, for
example), and everyone with an e-mail address from that organization
will be able to send documents to your Kindle as long as they have its
e-mail address. Click Add Address, and you're ready to send e-mails to
your Kindle from that address.

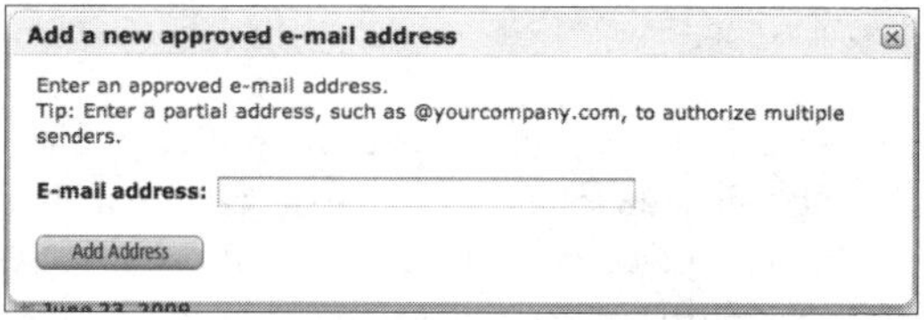

Figure 6.3

*Type an address
and click Add
Address. If you
want to approve
a whole e-mail
domain, type
@thedomain.com.*

Add a new approved e-mail address   ☒

Enter an approved e-mail address.
Tip: Enter a partial address, such as @yourcompany.com, to authorize multiple
senders.

E-mail address: [   ]

[Add Address]

E-mailing Your Documents

You know how to send e-mails, so I am not going to go into the nitty-
gritty of composing e-mails. However, you do need to know the e-mail
address of your Kindle. On your Fire, tap Docs on the home screen to go
to your Personal Documents library (**Figure 6.4**). Your Fire's e-mail address
is displayed front and center.

Figure 6.4

Your Docs library is stored on your device, so everything in it takes up space on your Fire.

Open your e-mail program of choice, and using an e-mail account on the approved list, compose a new e-mail to your Fire's e-mail address. A subject line isn't needed, nor is any text in the body of the e-mail, just attachments.

Here are a couple of notes:

- The maximum file size allowed for use with Kindle Personal Documents Service is 50MB.

- PDF support is "experimental." Simple PDFs should convert without a problem, but you might notice some funkiness (that's a technical term) with converted PDFs that have complex layouts or lots of graphics.

- You can attach up to 25 documents to one e-mail for converting.

- If you like to compress things, you can zip all your documents together and send the .zip file to your Kindle's e-mail address.

Once you have your e-mail composed, with your attachments attached, hit Send. It'll take a few minutes (slightly longer for PDFs) for your documents to show up on your Kindle. When they are ready, they are automatically added to your Docs library on your Fire.

Tap the document to read it, using the same controls and options that are available when you're reading a book on your Kindle (see Chapter 3 for more information).

The Special Case of PDFs

PDFs are great because they are a faithful representation of the layout of the original document. No matter what computer/device you're using, as long as it supports PDFs, that document will look the same.

The Fire natively supports PDFs, meaning that when you transfer a PDF to your Fire using the Kindle Personal Documents Service, you're basically e-mailing the PDF to your Kindle. Unlike Kindle-format books, you can't change the font size or typeface of a PDF. If the font is tiny, you'll just have to pinch and zoom to read it.

The Kindle Personal Documents Service can, however, convert PDFs to Kindle format when you transfer them via e-mail. This way, you can adjust fonts and margins like you can on any Kindle book. Simply attach the PDF, or PDFs, to an e-mail addressed to your Fire, and type **convert** for the subject. This tells the service to convert the attached PDF and then deliver it to your Docs library in Kindle format.

USB

If e-mail isn't your thing or you don't have access to an e-mail account but you do have a computer and a mini-USB cable (I know that seems unlikely, but you never know), you can transfer personal documents to your Fire manually. Keep in mind that since you aren't using the Kindle Personal Documents Service, you don't get all the added benefits like syncing notes. Also, any documents transferred to a Fire in this manner will be available only on that specific Fire.

Take your trusty mini-USB cable and plug it into your computer and your Fire. Unlock your Fire, and it will be in USB mode. A drive called Kindle will appear on your computer. Double-click it, and you'll see a bunch of directories. This is where your Kindle stores your stuff (the stuff that's on the device at least). The folder you're looking for is called Documents.

Drag your .pdf, .mobi, .azm, and text files into that folder. Once you're finished, tap Disconnect on the Fire's screen, and your files will be in your Docs library.

Using Docs

Now that you've filled your Fire up with files, it is time to dive into some of them. Tap Docs on the home screen, and you're taken to your personal Docs (shown in Figure 6.4). This is the only one of your Fire's content libraries that doesn't have a Cloud library and a Device library. All of the documents in the Docs library, even the ones transferred using the Kindle Personal Documents Service, are stored locally on the device.

Just like you can with any other piece of content, you can add Docs to your Favorites. Long tap one to bring up the contextual menu (**Figure 6.5**). Select Add to Favorites, and it'll be added. You can also delete documents by selecting Delete.

Figure 6.5
The contextual menu allows you to add a personal document to your Favorites or delete it.

The Docs library has all the features of the other libraries. You can search for documents by typing in the Search box at the top of the library. You can switch between grid and list views by tapping the menu icon in the options bar, and you can sort your documents via Docs by Recent (the most recently added/used displayed first) or by Title (alphabetical by title).

To open a Doc, just tap it. If the Doc is a Kindle book or a converted PDF, the controls are the same as when you're reading a book.

If you're reading a nonconverted PDF, things are a little different. Turning the pages is the same: Tap the right side of the screen to advance and the left to go back (and you can also swipe to turn the page). However, when you tap the middle of the screen to bring up the options bar, you'll notice a decided lack of options (**Figure 6.6**). All you have is a slider to go forward or back in the PDF and the home and back icons. As I mentioned, when reading a PDF, you have no control over the way it looks: You can't increase the font or anything of the like. You can pinch to zoom in the document, however, so if the font is too small on the screen, just pinch until your eyes are comfortable.

Figure 6.6

The options available when reading a PDF are pretty sparse. You have the location slider and home and back buttons, and that's it.

Apps

Apps, short for "applications," are everywhere nowadays: on your phone, on your fridge, in your car, and on your Kindle Fire. Apps are programs that add functionality. This functionality can be something related to your job, such as giving your Kindle the ability to open Office documents, or something fun, such as the countless games available for your Fire.

A wide variety of apps are available for sale on the Amazon Appstore that you can purchase right from your Fire. Prices do vary, but I'll show you how you can try selected apps without having to spend a dime.

This chapter covers how to use the Amazon Appstore on your Fire and on Amazon.com, how to launch apps, and how to manage your app collection.

Built-in Apps

On your home screen, tap Apps on the navigation bar, and you'll enter your Apps library (**Figure 7.1**). All your apps purchased from Amazon are listed in the Cloud library; on-device apps are in the Device library.

Figure 7.1
The Cloud and Device Apps libraries

Every Fire owner gets access to the following apps in their Cloud library automatically:

- *Gallery*: This app displays any photos or videos you transfer to your Fire.

- *Shop*: Shop Amazon.com right on your Fire with this app.

- *Contacts*: You can add contact information for various people to this app.

- *Email*: Check your e-mail on your Fire (see the next section for more details).

- *Facebook*: This isn't actually an app; rather, it is a link to Facebook's mobile website.

- *Help & Feedback*: Find help for troubleshooting your Fire with this app.

- *IMDb*: This is the app companion to the movie-tracking website of the same name.

- *Pulse*: You can keep up with the news in a highly visual fashion with this app.

Apps that haven't been installed from the Cloud library have an arrow in the lower-right corner of their icon (see the Documents app in Figure 7.1).

To install an app, tap it. You're taken to that app's page on the Amazon Appstore (**Figure 7.2**). Tap the orange install button, and the app is downloaded from the cloud. Upon successful installation, a notification is displayed. Tap the notification to launch the app, or ignore it and continue to install other apps.

Figure 7.2
Installing an app from the cloud requires just a couple of clicks.

The newly installed app is now listed in your Device library as well as the Cloud library. Tap the icon to launch the app (**Figure 7.3**). Thousands of apps are available for your Fire, so it would be impossible for me to explain how to use all of those apps in this book. However, there is one tip you should know.

Figure 7.3
Fruit Ninja is a full-screen game. Tap the triangle at the bottom of the screen to bring up the options and status bars.

As you can see in Figure 7.3, I'm about to play a game of Fruit Ninja (fun game, by the way). Notice the arrow at the bottom of the screen. Some apps, especially games, use your Fire's entire screen. This isn't a problem, but you need a way to get to the options bar so you can go back to your home screen. Other full-screen activities on the Fire, such as reading a book or watching a movie, solve this problem by hiding the controls until you tap the middle of the screen. This isn't an option for other apps because that tap could be used for some important app-related function.

Tapping the arrow at the bottom of the screen reveals the options and status bars.

Email App

One Fire app deserves a dedicated section: Email. Tap the Email app to launch it. If this is the first time launching Email, setup begins automatically (**Figure 7.4**). Tap Start, and select the type of e-mail account you're setting up (I'm going with Gmail) (**Figure 7.5**).

Figure 7.4
The e-mail setup welcome screen

Figure 7.5
If your e-mail provider is listed, the server settings are automatically entered for you.

No matter which account type you select, next you need to enter your username (e-mail address) and password. Tap Next, and if you're setting up an AOL, Yahoo!, Google, or Hotmail e-mail account, the server settings are detected automatically.

If, however, you're setting up another kind of e-mail account, you'll need to provide the server settings. Check with your e-mail service provider for the proper settings of your account (Exchange support isn't on the Fire natively, but many apps in the store support this type of corporate mail).

Once you've applied the server settings, type a display name (this is the name that will be displayed on e-mails you send) and a name for the account (**Figure 7.6**). By default this e-mail account is set as your main account. Any e-mail sent from the Kindle will come from this account. You can also choose to import your contacts at this point.

Figure 7.6
Display Name determines how your name appears on e-mails from your Fire; Account name is optional and is displayed only on your Fire.

Viewing and Reading E-mails

The Email app should be familiar to anyone who has used an e-mail client (**Figure 7.7** on the next page). Your inbox is displayed by default with unread messages in bold white and read messages grayed out. You can flag messages by tapping the flag icon, and if you swipe to the right

on a message, checkboxes appear, with the swiped message selected
(**Figure 7.8**). Tap the checkboxes to select more messages and then tap one
of the action buttons to select Mark as Read/Unread, Move, or Delete.

Figure 7.7
*The inbox with
the menu button
tapped*

Figure 7.8
*Select an e-mail
to mark as
read, move it, or
delete it.*

You can change the sorting of messages by tapping the top-right menu
and selecting a new sort order (**Figure 7.9**).

Figure 7.9
*The sort options
available in the
e-mail app*

To read an e-mail message, tap it (**Figure 7.10**). The options bar has a menu button that lets you mark the message as unread, move it to another folder, or mark it as spam. You can also reply by tapping the reply arrow (at the right end of the options bar), delete the message by tapping the trash can, or create an entirely new message by tapping the square icon with a pencil in it.

Figure 7.10
*Reading an
e-mail on the Fire*

 It is possible to save attachments to your Fire, so you can use e-mail as another way to get content onto your Fire.

Tap the menu button in the options bar to add another account by tapping the account button, or tap the folders button to view another folder in your e-mail account (shown in Figure 7.7). You can also see some e-mail help, view your contacts (if you imported them), and check out the mail settings.

The settings allow you to set how often your mail is checked (by default it is a manual process), set an e-mail signature (by default the signature is "Sent from my Kindle Fire"), and more.

Composing E-mails

Tapping the new e-mail button opens the compose screen (**Figure 7.11** on the next page). Type an e-mail address (or addresses) in the To field, type a subject and a message, and hit Send.

Figure 7.11
Composing an e-mail on the Fire is pretty much like composing an e-mail on any other device.

You can also attach files by tapping the Attach button. As you can see, you have to pick an app and then select files from within that app to attach to your e-mail (**Figure 7.12**).

Figure 7.12
You can attach files from certain apps to an e-mail.

Getting Apps

You can get apps onto your Kindle Fire in three ways: from Amazon.com, from the Amazon Appstore on the Fire, and by "sideloading" them.

Amazon, much like Apple and Google, runs a store full of both free and paid apps. Amazon approves all of apps in its app store. This allows Amazon to make sure malicious and pointless apps stay out of the store and that only apps worth your time, and money, are available. *Sideloading* allows you to install apps onto your Fire manually from somewhere other than Amazon, which has some benefits and downsides.

Amazon.com

You can reach the Amazon Appstore on your computer by pointing your browser of choice to *http://amazon.com/appstore* (**Figure 7.13**). The Amazon Appstore lists a number of different apps for sale, in a variety of categories. You can search it just as you would any part of Amazon or browse by clicking the links in the left navigation.

Figure 7.13
The Amazon Appstore on Amazon.com

Once you find an app you like, click it to see details (**Figure 7.14** on the next page). The app's icon is displayed along with the name, the rating, and the price (in red). If you scroll down, you'll see the typical Amazon.com details page listing other apps you might like if you are interested in this one, reviews, and product details.

Figure 7.14
A detail page for the Wolfram|Alpha app on Amazon.com

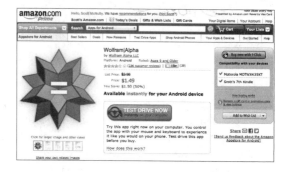

Check out the green section with the "Buy now..." button. Under that button the device compatibility of this app is listed. I happen to have two devices registered with my Amazon account that are compatible with the Amazon Appstore: a Motorola phone and my Kindle Fire (called "Scott's 7th Kindle"). In Figure 7.14 you can tell that the Wolfram|Alpha app is supported on both my Android phone and the Fire. If the Fire weren't supported, there would be an *X* next to it (**Figure 7.15**). The app won't work on your Fire, but you can still purchase it if you like.

Figure 7.15
If the app isn't compatible with your Fire, an x is displayed next to it in the Device list.

One of the greatest things about the Amazon Appstore is that big green Test Drive Now button in Figure 7.14. You can try selected apps in your browser before you decide to spend your hard-earned money on it. Click the Test Drive Now button, and a simulated phone appears with the app running on it (**Figure 7.16**). You can change the orientation of the phone by clicking the orientation icon in the lower-left corner and type by clicking into text fields and using your keyboard. Once you're done with your test-drive (you are limited to 30 minutes), click the Close button to return to the app's detail page.

Figure 7.16
Test-driving an app on Amazon.com

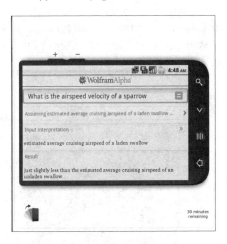

Tap the "Buy it now..." button to purchase the app (yes, even if the app is free, you're still "purchasing" it). The app will now appear in your Fire's Cloud library just waiting for you to install it (**Figure 7.17**).

Figure 7.17
Apps purchased on the Web automatically appear in your Cloud library.

Fire

If you have your Kindle Fire handy, it makes sense to do your app shopping on the device. Not only is the store formatted for the Fire's screen, but it also shows you only apps that are Fire-compatible.

Tap the Store button, and you're taken to the Amazon Appstore front page (**Figure 7.18**). Displayed front and center is another one of the Amazon Appstore's greatest features: the free app of the day.

Figure 7.18
The Amazon Appstore on your Fire

Every day Amazon takes a paid app and makes it free to download. This is a great way to build your Fire's Apps library with high-quality apps without breaking the bank.

Below the free app of the day are the various categories in the Amazon Appstore. Below the categories are two lists: the top 100 most downloaded free and paid apps (free on the right, paid on the left). The app's icon, name, maker, rating, and price are all displayed. Swipe up with your finger to scroll through the list and browse for apps.

You can also browse by category. Swipe your finger across the category bar to scroll through; then tap a category to see all the apps within (**Figure 7.19**). The apps are sorted by relevance. Tap the Refine button to change the sorting method and filter results (available filters are price, release date, and rating).

Figure 7.19
You can browse apps by category.

Next to the All button are two other ways to view the apps in this category: Top and Recommended For You. Tapping Top displays the most popular apps in the category, and tapping Recommended For You displays the apps Amazon thinks you might be interested in.

Once you've found an app you want, simply tap it to see the details page (**Figure 7.20** on the next page). The app's icon is displayed to the left with some details about the app and three buttons: an orange button with the price of the app (free in this case), Save, and Share. Tapping the Save button adds the app to your Saved for Later list, which is a great way to keep a tally of apps you're interested in without buying/downloading them.

Figure 7.20
The detail page of an app in the store

Tapping Share brings up the Share this app menu, with a number of different options depending on the apps you have installed on your Fire (**Figure 7.21**). If you have a Twitter app installed, or other sharing app, there would be more options here.

Figure 7.21
Depending on your apps, you may be able to share a link to an app in a variety of ways. I can only send an e-mail.

Tapping the orange button turns it into a green Get App button. Tap it again to actually purchase the app and start the download process.

There isn't a way to try an app for free on your Fire, but if you aren't sure whether this is the app for you, the detail page has some more information to help you decide. The Product Info section lists a description provided by the creator of the app. Scroll with your finger to see the list of application permission (**Figure 7.22**). This explicitly lists what this particular app can and can't access on your Fire, which is always nice to know. At the very bottom of the screen the file size of the app is listed, and there is a Report an Issue with this App button.

Figure 7.22

When you install an app, you're giving it permission to access your information. Application Permissions shows you exactly what an app can do on your Fire.

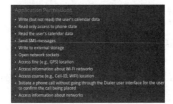

If you notice an app doing something it shouldn't or if it crashes over and over again, tap this button, and a menu of reasons will appear. Select your reason for being unhappy with the app, and you're presented with a form to fill out fully describing your grievances (AccuWeather for Android is a fine app; I'm just using it as an example) (**Figure 7.23**).

Figure 7.23

If you experience issues with an app, you can report it to Amazon using this form.

The Photos section displays screenshots of the app to give you an idea of what the app will look like on your Fire. The photos are displayed full-screen, so it is a pretty good approximation of the app (without all that pesky functionality to cloud your judgment). Reviews from users are available by tapping Reviews, and you can even create your own review after you've installed the app (**Figure 7.24**).

Figure 7.24
People who have bought/downloaded an app can leave a review. You can even do it right from your Fire.

Finally, the Recommendations section lists apps other people who viewed the current app actually purchased (**Figure 7.25**).

Figure 7.25
Want some more apps like the one you're looking at? Recommendations lists similar apps.

If you still can't find the app you're looking for, tap the search icon in the options bar and type a query. A list of apps will be returned that match what you are looking for. You'll find the options bar at the bottom of the Amazon Appstore screen.

Tap the menu button to see six buttons (**Figure 7.26**):

Figure 7.26
The menu options in the Amazon Appstore

- *Categories*: Tapping this brings up a list of the app categories. Tap the category to see all the apps in the list.

- *Recommended*: This is a list of apps Amazon thinks you might like.

- *My Subscriptions*: Some magazines are available as apps instead of Kindle magazines. This section allows you to manage those particular subscription settings.

- *My Apps*: This is a list of all the apps you're purchased from the Amazon Appstore (**Figure 7.27**). The interesting thing about this list, though, is the Update Available button. Tap it to see a list of all the apps on your Fire that have an update you can apply.

Figure 7.27
My Apps lists all the apps you've obtained from Amazon, as well as any apps that require an update.

- *Settings*: This opens the Amazon Appstore settings (**Figure 7.28** on the next page). You can apply a gift card or check your balance here.

Figure 7.28

The Amazon Appstore settings allow you to check gift card balances, enable parental controls, and disable in-app purchasing.

Some apps allow you to purchase content inside the app itself, such as additional levels in a game or magazine subscriptions. Enabling Parental Controls requires your Amazon account password, or a PIN, be entered whenever an in-app purchase is made (so your kids can't go crazy and spend all your money on virtual goods).

- *More*: More is a sort of grab bag (**Figure 7.29**). Here you can access your Saved for Later apps. You can also see a list of your Recently Viewed apps, in case you vaguely recall looking at a cool app but you can't remember its name. Rounding out the options are a couple of ways to get help (Contact Customer Service, Help), leave feedback, and review the legal terms of service for the Amazon Appstore.

Figure 7.29

Tapping More brings up a list of additional things including the Saved for Later list.

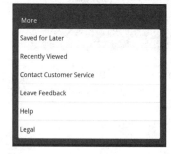

Sideloading

The last method of getting apps onto your Fire is a little more involved than just tapping a couple of buttons. The Fire, by default, installs only those apps from the Amazon Appstore, but there are a number of other Android stores out there (including the Google Marketplace, which is the standard app store for most other Android devices).

note As a quick reminder, the operating system that your Fire runs is called Android. Google developed it as an open source operating system, and Amazon heavily modified it to create the user experience currently on your Fire.

It is possible to install, or *sideload*, apps from other app stores onto your Fire. Why would you want to do this? As I mentioned earlier, any app in the Amazon Appstore is there because Amazon approved it. This means some apps aren't in the store because Amazon rejected them or the developer didn't want to list them in the Amazon Appstore for whatever reason. You can install an app like this on your Fire; it just requires more work.

First you need to enable sideloading. Tap the Quick Settings icon in the status menu (the gear) > More > Device. Turn on Allow Installation of Applications From Unknown Sources (which sounds more ominous than sideloading) (**Figure 7.30**). A warning pops up letting you know that Amazon takes no responsibility for any damage you may do to your Kindle with these crazy apps. Tap OK, and now you can sideload all the apps you want.

Figure 7.30
Turn on Allow Installation of Applications From Unknown Sources to enable side-loading of apps.

Every app on your Fire is just a collection of files grouped together into another file called an .apk file. To sideload an app, you need to first find the app's .apk file. Some Android app developers allow you to directly download the .apk file from their websites (Firefox does) though most don't. The easiest way to get your hands on the .apk file for a particular app is to install it on another Android device that supports the store it is from and then back up the file using a backup app to your computer or another form of removable media.

Once you have the .apk file on your computer, connect your Kindle Fire to your computer using a micro-USB cable. Unlock the Fire, and it'll be in USB drive mode. The Kindle drive will appear either on your Desktop (Mac) or in the Windows Explorer. Double-click the Kindle drive and create a new directory (I would call is something like CustomApps). Drag and drop the .apk files into your new directory.

Disconnect your Fire and go to the Amazon Appstore. Look for a file browser app that will allow you to look at all the files on your Fire, including the .apk you just copied into that special directory. Install whichever one you like the best. Launch the file browser and locate the .apk. Tap it, and the app will install itself to your Device library.

Note that apps installed this way aren't guaranteed to work at all and will not receive updates automatically.

Managing Your Apps

Long tapping any of your apps allows you to add it to your home screen Favorites or remove it/install it (Device library and Cloud library apps, respectively), but that is not the limit to which you can manage your apps (**Figure 7.31**).

Figure 7.31
The app contextual menu includes Add to Favorites, Remove from Device, and Install (for apps in the Cloud).

Tap Quick Settings > More > Applications, and you'll see a list of all the running apps on your Fire. The drop-down at the top allows you to switch the view to only third-party apps or all apps on the Fire (**Figure 7.32**).

Figure 7.32
The Applications screen can display all currently running apps, just third-party apps, or all the apps on your device.

Tap an app to see your options (**Figure 7.33**). From here you can quit an app if it is running down your battery or erase all the data it is storing to free up space. You can also uninstall the app completely with a tap.

Figure 7.33

Tapping an app on the Applications screen gives you access to the Force Stop, Uninstall, and Clear Data functions.

8

Web

The Fire is a great device for web browsing. I find myself using it more and more for casual Internet surfing as I watch TV. Fire's browser, Silk, offers up all the features we have come to expect from a modern browser: tabs, bookmarks, and integrated Google search. The most interesting feature of Silk isn't on your Fire at all; it is in the cloud.

Amazon calls it *accelerated browsing*. As mentioned in Chapter 1, when you open a website in Silk, you're actually telling some of Amazon's servers to fetch the page for it, do whatever processing is required, and deliver the page to your Fire. Offloading the crunching of scripts and other potentially processor-intensive tasks has two effects: It allows your Fire to use its processor power for other tasks, and it speeds up your web browsing.

This chapter covers how to browse with Silk, how to use bookmarks, and how to turn off accelerated browsing.

Browsing the Web

You won't find the name Silk anywhere on your Fire. Instead, the browser is simply referenced as Web. Tap the Web button on the navigation bar of the home screen to open Silk (**Figure 8.1**). Silk opens a tab displaying thumbnail images of your bookmarked and recently visited sites. Tap a thumbnail to load that page in the browser.

Figure 8.1
Silk, the Fire's web browser, is fully featured.

At the top of the screen is the tab bar. All tabs with pages loaded in them appear across here with the title of the website displayed at the top (in

Figure 8.1 the tab is labeled New Tab because there isn't a page loaded).
Tap a tab to switch to it. When you get more than a handful of tabs open,
you'll need to swipe through the list.

Under the tab bar is the URL field just waiting for you to start typing in a
URL. Tap the URL field and start typing (**Figure 8.2**). As you type, Silk does
four neat things to save you some typing time:

Figure 8.2

*You can type
either URLs or
web searches
here.*

- Based on what you're typing, it suggests a number of Google searches
  you might be interested in.

- Using Google, Silk tries to predict the URL you're typing and displays
  some potential matches.

- Silk searches your browsing history and displays past pages you've
  visited that match what you're typing.

- Silk searches your bookmarks and displays matches.

The suggestions are displayed together in a list. Each suggestion has a
different icon so you can tell them apart: URLs have a globe icon, searches
get a magnifying glass icon, History results display a clock icon, and bookmarks include the bookmark icon. If one of them actually matches what
you're looking for, tap it to save yourself some typing.

Above the keyboard you'll also find that Silk is attempting to guess which URL you are typing (shown in Figure 8.2). If you're interested in one of the suggestions, tap it, and the URL will be filled in.

At the bottom of the screen you'll find our old friend the options bar with home, back, forward, menu, and bookmark buttons. Tap the menu button to bring up the options:

- *Add bookmark*: Tap this button while you're on a page to add it to your bookmarks.

- *History*: To view your browsing history, tap this button, and you'll see a list of sites you've recently visited (**Figure 8.3**).

Figure 8.3
History keeps track of where you've been.

- *Share page*: While on a page, tap this button to send the URL you're looking at to one of the listed apps (**Figure 8.4**).

Figure 8.4
Sharing a link from Silk is as easy as tapping the Share button and selecting a method of sharing.

- *Downloads*: You can download files from the Web using Silk. Download progress is listed here.

- *Find in page*: Looking for a particular word on a page? Tap this button and enter the word, or phrase, you're looking for, and matches are highlighted (**Figure 8.5**). Tap the arrows to cycle through the matches.

Figure 8.5
In-page search helps you find exactly what you're looking for.

- *Settings*: Silk has lots of settings you can fiddle with; tap here and start tweaking.

As you're browsing around, you'll want to open additional tabs. Tap the + icon at the upper-right corner to open a new tab, and you can load another page.

Long tap a tab to bring up three options: "Close tab," "Close other tabs," and "Close all tabs" (**Figure 8.6**). I've found "Close other tabs" especially useful in my browsing.

Figure 8.6
Long tap a tab to bring up this menu.

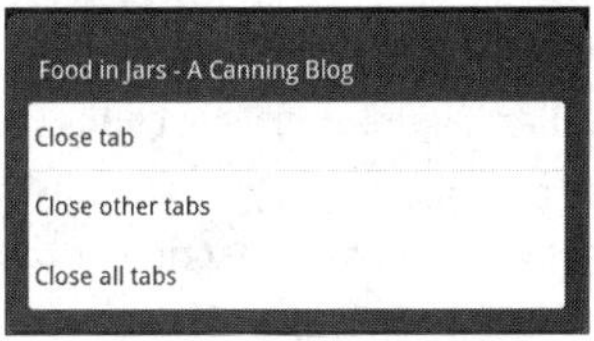

Food in Jars - A Canning Blog

Close tab

Close other tabs

Close all tabs

You can also long tap a link on any page to bring up even more options:

- *Open*: Opens the link in your current tab.

- *Open in new tab*: Opens the link in a new tab.

- *Bookmark link*: Adds a bookmark for the selected tab.

- *Save link*: Downloads the link to your Fire. This is useful for PDFs, e-books, and the like.

- *Copy link URL*: Copies the selected link's URL so you can paste it into the URL field or an e-mail.

- *Share link*: Brings up the same share menu shown in Figure 8.5.

Silk allows you to save images from websites to the Gallery app. Long tap an image you would like to save, and a menu appears (**Figure 8.7**). Tap "Save image" to save it to the Gallery app, and tap "View image" to open it in a new tab.

Figure 8.7
Want to save an image from the Web to the Gallery app? Long tap and select "Save image."

Setting Bookmarks

Bookmarks allow you to save a website to a list for easy access later (which you probably already knew). When you're browsing the Web using Silk and you want to save a site to your bookmarks, just tap the bookmark icon in the options bar (**Figure 8.8**). This opens your bookmarks, which can be displayed in one of two ways: grid or list view (**Figure 8.9**). Grid view lists all your bookmarks as a collection of thumbnails. List view is more compact, displaying your bookmarks as a text list with the name of the website along with the URL shown.

Figure 8.8
The humble book-mark icon waiting to be tapped

Figure 8.9
Bookmarks viewed two ways: grid view on top and list view on the bottom

 tip You can toggle between the two views by tapping the icon at the top right of the bookmarks screen.

No matter which view you use, the first item will allow you to add the page you're currently on to your bookmarks. In grid view, the first thumbnail is an image of the page you were just viewing with a black plus sign superimposed over it. The first item in list view is "Add bookmark" (in orange text) with the URL beneath it. Tapping either opens the "Add bookmark" menu (**Figure 8.10**). The name and URL are both pulled from the website, but you can customize either by tapping in the field and typing something.

Once you're happy with the information in the fields, tap the OK button, and the site is bookmarked (tap Cancel if you've changed your mind). Now that site is only a couple taps away.

To edit a bookmark, long tap it in the bookmarks screen. A menu appears with a few options; the one you're interested in is "Edit bookmark." Tapping "Edit bookmark" opens the "Add bookmark" menu (shown in Figure 8.10) where you can change the name or URL to anything you like.

Figure 8.10
When adding a bookmark, you can assign it a custom name.

To delete a bookmark, long tap and then tap Delete. A warning appears asking you to confirm that you want to delete the bookmark. Tap OK, and the bookmark is gone.

> **tip** You can also bookmark sites from the History screen. Tap the menu button and select History. Next to each item in your History is a bookmark icon (Figure 8.11). Tap it, and that site is bookmarked. Tap again, and it is removed.

Figure 8.11
The bookmark icon in History enables you to quickly bookmark sites.

Silk Settings

Silk has a bunch of settings that control everything from the size of the text (options bar > menu button > Settings > Text size in General

Settings) to blocking pop-up windows (the last item in the Behavior section) (**Figure 8.12**). I won't bore you by going through all the available settings, but I do want to highlight a few:

Figure 8.12
A small sampling of Silk's settings

- *Set search engine*: Not a fan of Google? You can change the search engine Silk uses to either Bing or Yahoo!

- *Clear all cookie data, Clear cache, and Clear history*: These are three separate settings, but when used in combination, they basically reset your entire browsing history.

- *Enable plug-ins*: The Fire comes with Adobe Flash installed, which means you can watch Flash videos with Silk. The performance isn't great, sadly, so you might want to disable plug-ins or set it to "On demand" so that Flash is used only when needed.

- *Accelerate page loading*: By default this option is enabled. Turn this off if you don't like the idea of almost all of your web traffic going through Amazon's servers (secure connections using SSL bypass Amazon's servers even when this is enabled). You can always turn it back on again after you examine Amazon's privacy policy. See "Browsing with Silk and the Cloud" in Chapter 1 for more details.

Index